THE
BIG BOOK OF
CHESS

THE
BIG BOOK OF

CHESS

ERIC SCHILLER

CARDOZA
PUBLISHING

Cardoza Publishing is the foremost gaming publisher in the world, with a library of over 175 up-to-date and easy-to-read books and strategies. These authoritative works are written by the top experts in their fields and with more than 8,500,000 books in print, represent the best-selling and most popular gaming books anywhere.

FIRST EDITION

Library of Congress Catalog Card No: 2003113829
ISBN: 1-58042-133-4

Visit our web site—www.cardozapub.com—or write
for a full list of books and computer strategies.

CARDOZA PUBLISHING
P.O. Box 1500, Cooper Station, New York, NY 10276
Phone (800) 577-WINS
email: cardozapub@aol.com

DEDICATION

The game of chess has often provided distraction and relief in troubled times. I had originally intended to dedicate this book to the people of the city of Baghdad, which was at one time the chess capital of the world. As I was writing this book, however, the great tragedy of the tsunami occurred. So I dedicate this book to those still suffering because of all of the unfortunate circumstances surrounding the events of late 2004. I hope that chess may bring some comfort, or at least necessary distraction, in such difficult times.

This book contains information I have gathered over the course of four decades of playing chess and studying the game. Most of this information comes from the vast sea of chess literature. Near the end of the book, you'll find a section of recommended reading that includes the primary sources I used for writing this book. The body of knowledge accumulated makes chess one of the most thoroughly studied human activities. Countless writers and researchers have toiled away to create this wonderful body of literature. They all deserve thanks and credit for bringing these facts into the historical record.

A number of individuals contributed to directly or indirectly, or inspired, some of the material presented in this book. I thank Maurice Ashley, Pavel Blatny, Hal Bogner, Graham Clayton, Calvin Duif, Chris Duncan, Andrzej Filipowicz, Ray Keene, Stewart Reuben, Tony Saidy, and John Watson for helpful ideas and discussion. Thanks, too, to Fernando Rodriguez, Carla Hummel, Elizabeth Karnazes, Ratko Knezevic, Richard Shorman, Academic Chess, ChessDryad (www.chessdryad.com) and the Long Island Chess Museum (www.clipart.co.uk) for photos.

The quotations presented come from a wide variety of sources, including a variety of web sites. I found the Kent Chess page (www.kentchess.org/links/quotations.htm) to be very helpful, and also the Chessville site (www.chessville.com/misc/Quotes/misc_trivia_quotes_misc.htm).

The dedicated staff of Cardoza Publishing, who had to oversee the complicated process of putting this book together, have my eternal thanks.

A wonderful team examined the book at proof stage and made valuable contributions pointing out errors. Cardoza Publishing joins me in thanking Erin Dame, Carl Palmateer, Joe Williams, Warren Norred, James Sampatra, and Scott Thompson.

CONTENTS

INTRODUCTION 13

CHAPTER 1 The Ultimate Mind Sport 15

Why Do People Play Chess? 16
Where Did Chess Come From? 22
Baghdad in the Eighth Century 23
The Conquest of Europe 25
Globalization 26

CHAPTER 2 Rankings for All 29

International Titles 31
World Championship 32
The Chess Olympics 34
Show Me the Money! 36
The HB Global Chess Challenge Prize Fund 37
Betting on Chess 39

CHAPTER 3 A Few Chess FAQs 41

Do You Have to be a Nerd to Play Chess? 41
Does Chess Really Improve Academic Test Results? 42
Do You Have to Be a Genius to Be a Chess Master? 42
Can You Play Chess in Jail? 43
Can Chess Be Dangerous? 44
A Question for You 45

CHAPTER 4 Ready to Play 47

The Basic Rules of the Game 47
The Battlefield 48
The Forces 49
The King 50
The Rook 54
The Bishop 55
The Queen 56
The Knight 58
The Pawn 59
Promotion 65
Summary of Pawn Moves 68
Check 69
Checkmate 73
Castling 74
Quiz on the Rules 80
How Much is Each Piece Worth? 84

Win, Lose, or Draw? 86

    How to Win (or Lose) the Game 87

    Checkmate Brings Victory 88

    Your First Checkmate Strategy 99

    How to Lose Quickly at Chess 101

    How Games are Drawn 103

    How to Offer a Draw 104

CHAPTER 5 Advanced Rules for Tournament Play — 107

The Arbiter 107

Touch-Move 111

    J'adoube! 111

Notation 112

    The Scoresheet 120

Time Controls 121

    Standard Time Control 122

    Amateur Time Control 124

    Blitz Chess 124

CHAPTER 6 The Opening — 125

Starting the Game 126

    The Names of the Openings 127

Four Keys to Open the Game 128

    Seize the Center 128

    Castling to Safety 129

    Connecting the Rooks 130

    Further Adventures of the Rooks 130

    The Gambit 131

CHAPTER 7 The Middlegame — 135

When the Fight Is On, Tactics Rule! 136

    The Pin 136

    The Fork 141

    X-Ray 144

    Discovered Attack 145

    Discovered Check 147

    The Windmill 150

    Deflection and Decoy 155

    Obey the Labor Laws! 159

    There is No "Pass" in Chess 162

Four Keys to Tactical Thinking 165

    Capture-Checks 166

    Captures and Checks 171

Threats	177	
Improve a Piece's Position	178	
Planning and Plotting		**180**
Balance of Power	182	
Compensation	182	
Defense		**183**
King Safety	185	
Breathing Room	188	
The Walls (pawn structure)		**189**
Backward Pawns	189	
Doubled Pawns	190	
Triangles	191	
Holes	192	
The Isolated d-pawn	195	
Hanging Pawns	197	
Passed Pawns	198	
Pawn Chains	199	
Fun Along the Seventh Rank		**201**
Four Keys to Strategic Planning		**207**
Find the Weak Spots!	207	
Avoid Weaknesses	209	
Eliminate Defenders	210	
Capablanca's Rule	211	

CHAPTER 8 The Endgame — 213

Checkmate is the Goal		**214**
A New Queen is Crowned	214	
Escaping With a Draw	215	
Four Keys to the Endgame		**216**
Profit When you Trade!	217	
The Power of the King	218	
Eliminate the Last Pawn!	220	
When Desperate, Go for Stalemate.	220	

CHAPTER 9 The Sacrifice — 223

The Sicilian Offer You Can't Refuse	228	
Don't Look Greek Gift in the Mouth	229	
Breakthrough in the Endgame	231	
The Deep and True Sacrifice	233	
All for the Sake of Art		**239**
Chess Puzzles	240	
Endgame Studies	242	
Invented Games	242	

CHAPTER 10 Talk Like a Grandmaster 243

Where in the World is Kuala Lumpur?   244
New Kids on the Block   246

CHAPTER 11 Chess in the Major Leagues 247

The Round Robin Tournament   248
The Swiss System Tournament   252
The Knockout Competition   258
Patrons and Sponsors   258
The Press   260
Pomp and Circumstance   260
Team Chess   262
Drug Testing   263
Major Events in the Major Leagues   264

CHAPTER 12 Chess in the Minor Leagues 267

CHAPTER 13 Chess for John Q. Public 273

Chess in Schools   273
Chess Clubs   276
   America's Oldest Club: Mechanics'   276
   King's Head   277
Simultaneous Exhibitions   277
   Blindfold Simuls   279
   Postal Chess   280

CHAPTER 14 How to Behave 281

Professional Appearance   283
Spectators   285

CHAPTER 15 Tools of the Trade 291

Chess Equipment   291
   Buying a Chess Clock   291
Chess and Computers   292
   Chess-playing Software   292
   Chess Analysis Software   293
   Chess Instruction Software   294
   Playing Chess Online   294
Books and Multimedia   295
   Chess History   295
   All About the Openings   296
   Chess Strategy and Tactics   296

Relive Famous Tournaments   297
Getting up Close and Personal with the Players   298
On the Fringes   298
Chess Instruction   299
The Internet and World Wide Web   301

CHAPTER 16 Closing Thoughts   305

INDEX   307

INTRODUCTION

Chess is a sea in which a gnat may drink and an elephant may bathe.
—*Indian proverb*

My goal is to introduce you to "The Royal Game" — from the rules and some of its leading players to the exotic locales where chess is a part of daily life. I hope that you will share my fascination with the game after you have traveled through the pages of the *Big Book of Chess*.

This book is intended for easy reading, not as a reference work. I've included plenty of tips and advice on how to play well, but my main goal is to provide answers to the sorts of questions asked by beginning players and by those who are simply curious about chess and the people who play it.

I've been playing the game for many years, and enjoy it so much that I've written many books on the topic. I even spend my time teaching chess to others because I want them to appreciate chess the way I do. After reading this book, I hope you'll start to love chess, too.

I will cover many topics, from how the pieces move, to playing chess online. Please keep in mind that in this one book I can only scratch the surface of these many topics. I hope that when you finish reading it, you will go out and seek more information on the aspects of the game that have attracted your interest. Entire books, and even series of books, have been devoted to each of the topics I will mention. *The Big Book of Chess* will simply introduce you to the game and whet your appetite for more!

CHAPTER 1
The Ultimate Mind Sport

Chess is as much a mystery as women.
—*Cecil Purdy*

For centuries, chess has stood as the ultimate mind sport. The frequent references to chess in literature and movies are due to the general perception that anyone who plays chess must be intelligent. As a result, many writers include chess among the attributes of heroes and villains, to underscore their mental abilities.

Good vs. Bad in X-Men (© 20th Century Fox, 2000)

You might think that after all these years, some other game would rise up and knock chess off its esteemed pedestal, but chess has evolved into such a unique game that no other competitive mental activity can displace it.

Even before the very first international chess tournament over a century and a half ago, the results of chess games have been recorded. Thanks to the heroic work of chess fans all over the world, there are now databases containing not just the results, but every single move, of millions of chess games. Armed with this data, statisticians have worked out many interesting characteristics of the game of chess.

For example, the balance of the game is demonstrated by the winning percentage enjoyed by the player who has the privilege of moving first. It turns out that moving first is certainly an advantage, but not a great one. The player with the first move wins about 55 percent of the time. Chess games are not necessarily won or lost—quite often, neither player wins, and the result is a draw. In fact, about one-third of all chess games end in draws, with a higher ratio in professional competition and a much lower one in scholastic play.

The rules of the game have remained constant for the past few centuries, with only very minor modifications, mostly made to accommodate the use of chess clocks and the new digital timers. Of course, many changes have been proposed, and a huge number of chess variants exist with altered rules, different kinds of moves for pieces, differently shaped chess boards, and other variations. Still, despite passionate and sometimes professional promotion, not a single one of these variants has gathered any significant international following. Most of the variants are short-lived, and for good reason. It seems that designing another board game with the balance, elegance, and staying power of chess is beyond the reach of mere mortals. It has taken over a thousand years to perfect this magnificent game, and it remains the most popular. No other strategy game comes close to its ubiquitousness. Even in the electronic gaming age, chess remains the number one game in the world.

Why Do People Play Chess?

Chess is so interesting in itself, that those who have leisure for such diversions cannot find one that is more innocent, but advantageous, to the vanquished as well as the victor.
– Benjamin Franklin

People have been drawn to the game of chess for at least 1,500 years. It is the second most popular sport in the world, trailing only soccer. There must be something about the game that attracts such a passionate and devoted following.

Since chess is not an athletic sport, competition is open to everyone. Professional chess does require a great deal of stamina, and physical conditioning has become a great part of the modern chess scene. For casual play, however, it really doesn't matter what kind of physical shape you're in. Chess is even played by those who are blind and unable to see the board. Special chess sets allow them to play by touch, instead.

This non-reliance on physical strength or agility is one of the reasons why many find chess so appealing. Once you know how to play the game, you can look forward to playing it for the rest of your life. You won't have to give it up just because you grow old or ill. In fact, some grandmasters have been active on the professional scene into their 90s!

Of course, most people play chess because they find it fun and fascinating. I hope that as you read this book, you'll discover why. Let me point out a few reasons that people enjoy chess, sometimes to the point of addiction.

Intimate conversation without a word spoken; thrilling activity in quiescent; triumph and defeat, hope and despondency, life and death, all within 64 squares; poetry and signs reconciled; the ancient East at one with modern Europe—that is Chess.
—*John Holland Rose*

First, as with any other competitive activity, the thrill of victory provides a great feeling. Because chess is a purely mental contest with almost no element of luck involved, a person can take great pleasure in demonstrating prowess at the chessboard. But the greatest satisfaction is internal. It isn't just the pleasure that comes from making a brilliant move; it is the wonderful feeling that engulfs you as the correctness of your strategy permeates your consciousness. The feeling of discovery is a bit Zen-like—a sudden explosion filling the mind.

Second, since chess games in formal competition are recorded, and as I mentioned earlier, there are millions of them available, a chess game can earn a player a small slice of immortality. Every chess player dreams of playing some brilliant, never-before-seen strategy that will be admired throughout the world and will be referred to in newspaper columns and chess books as long as the game is played. Countless people are known to history only through some example of fantastic chess play that found its way into the chess community.

Everyone can define chess in their own way. But in the first place, chess is sport, because what we are really interested in is the name of the winner. However, I think that one's desire to win is not productive, unless it is grounded by one's striving to fight and to create something beautiful. But on the other hand, one can't be constantly winning when occupied with creating masterpieces. With me, however, as long as I have a desire to seek something new and to play beautiful games, I continue to win.
– *Garry Kasparov,* Thirteenth World Champion

Whether or not a player's impressive chess play finds its way into the data stream, it can still be fun to show off the move to others who play the game. They will be suitably impressed, and of course, that's a nice ego boost, too. In most sports and competitions, it is impossible to show off a move unless the highlight has been recorded on video. In chess, you can demonstrate exactly what happened in a game by simply setting up the chessboard and replaying the moves.

It is even possible to achieve chess immortality without playing a competitive game at all. Chess scholars analyze the commentaries of the great players, and often find some flaws. Although most of this work is now done with the assistance of powerful computer programs, lessening the originality of the new analysis, it is still possible to earn international recognition by pointing out errors in prominently published commentaries.

Since chess has existed for centuries, you may find it surprising that creativity and originality continue to play a large role in the game. The strategy of the first dozen or so moves of the chess game has still not been worked out with precision, even with all the computer assistance available. Every year, important new moves are still discovered even in the early stage of the game. Players and analysts can contribute important ideas in the opening, and they are rewarded by having their names attached to specific chess strategies.

♚ ♛ INFINITE VARIETY

There are more possible chess games available than there are electrons in the universe!

Another reason people enjoy chess is that, from a purely sporting standpoint, chess offers more opportunities for pulling off an upset than any other competition that does not involve a significant element of luck. Chess is such a complicated game that even the best players make some sort of mistake in almost every game. Often a player in a superior position will overplay the position and allow the opponent to strike back with a successful counterattack. Even the greatest chess players, including Bobby Fischer, have lost games to much less skilled opposition.

Did You Know?

The World Champion boxer Lennox Lewis is a big fan of the royal game. During the 2000 World Championship match in London, Lewis was training in England and very much wanted to come down and visit the match to see Kasparov and Kramnik in their title bout. However, his trainers said "no way," so he had to be content with reports from Roy Snell, the head of security of the chess match. Roy "Knuckles" Snell was actually a boxer himself, and he kept the world heavyweight champion informed about everything that was going on down in London.

"I honestly don't like him playing chess," said Emmanuel Steward, Lennox Lewis's trainer. "I mean, I see him sitting there for ten minutes thinking four moves ahead before he makes one. And he actually does the same thing in the ring—he thinks too much."

Informal competitions offer even greater chances to defeat a superior opponent. Professional players often give exhibitions, playing many opponents simultaneously. If you face off against a top professional who is facing fifteen or twenty opponents at the same time, you can devote that much more time to the analysis of the position. Sometimes even young children can defeat an experienced master under these circumstances.

Chess is one of the few activities in which players of all ages compete on a level playing field. At major open tournaments, you can find competitors as young as five years old and those who are well into their 90s. Hikaru Nakamura, still a junior, is now one of the top American players, having already won the U.S. Championship title. In the last century, Bobby Fischer won the United States championship at the tender age of fourteen. Hikaru is now a Grandmaster of chess, but he isn't nearly the youngest in the world. Later I'll go into more detail about the current record-holders.

For the most part, in chess competition boys, girls, men, and women all participate in the same section. There are specific championships for various age groups, and titles reserved for women, but in the overwhelming majority of events you'll find both men and women playing. This leads to many opportunities to make friends—and sometimes more romantic liaisons. Half a century ago, women were a rarity in professional chess. Now, women achieve impressive results in professional competition. Judit Polgar, who earned her Grandmaster title at age fifteen, is ranked solidly among the top ten players in the world.

Chess is also a great way to meet famous people. Many sports stars and celebrities enjoy chess, and often turn up at major professional chess events. Though most don't compete in tournaments, a large number of celebrities take private chess lessons and play with their friends and colleagues. Sometimes it can even become an obsession. For example, while filming *Around the World in Eighty Days*, Jackie Chan commented on "The Tonight Show" that whenever Arnold Schwarzenegger wasn't needed for a scene, the actor-turned-governor would sit in the corner playing chess. This is hardly a new phenomenon. Back in the golden days of Hollywood, Humphrey Bogart was an even more enthusiastic chess player, and quite a skilled one, too.

There have even been tournaments where only celebrities play. One such tournament was held in 1989 in the Mexican town of Mazatlan. Alongside this event, a World Championship of rapid chess took place. The chess stars and competing celebrities, including Morgan Fairchild, Erik Estrada and Claude Akins, mingled throughout the event.

During the 1993 United States Championship in Los Angeles, the hotel at which the event took place saw a massive influx of members of the World Wrestling Federation, who were about to perform in a nearby arena. To onlookers' amusement, the chess players and wrestlers were often found together in the bar.

The Phish Story

You might think it quite odd that a musical performance might be interrupted so that the musicians could take time out for a little chess, but it actually happened in quite spectacular fashion a few years ago. The immensely popular band Phish decided that they would feature chess on their 1995 tour by playing a chess game against the audience. The idea was that members of the audience could vote on a move during the intermission, and this move would be played on a giant demonstration board erected on stage. The band would then have until their next show to decide on their response.

I had been participating in the San Mateo International Futurity, an internationally ranked chess tournament featuring local masters, masters from Finland and Spain, and the most promising young stars from northern California.

With two tough games scheduled for Sunday, a night off at Shoreline Amphitheater seeing the brilliant and innovative group Phish seemed like the right way to relax before the difficult confrontation against a rising star whose national ranking was almost identical to my own. Since the pressure was on him to earn his international ranking, which I already had, I wanted to relax. Chess was the farthest from my mind as I entered the lawn to enjoy my first live Phish show.

What greeted me was a strange sight indeed. On the left side of the stage, there was a huge chessboard, with all the pieces in their proper places. I had no idea what was going on, but escaping from chess might prove to be impossible.

After the first two songs, the band explained what was going on. They are all big fans of the Royal Game and when they're on the road, they spend a lot of time doing battle at the chessboard. They would be challenging the audience to a game of chess on this national tour, with one move played at each concert.

During the set break, people were invited to gather at the Greenpeace booth and vote on the audience move. Of course I headed there, and introduced myself as a professional and the current champion of northern California. Many moves were suggested by the public. I explained why I felt that the choice should be between attacking the bishop with a pawn and bringing out the other knight. Eventually, the advance of the pawn from a7 to a6, kicking the bishop, was selected by vote.

I was then asked to make the move on the stage, which sounded like fun, so I readily agreed. I was escorted backstage where I met band members Page, Mike Gordon, Trey Anastasio, and Jon Fishman. They are genuine fans of chess, which I was very happy to discover, because chess suffers from such a geeky image that to find such terrific alternative musicians with a love for the game was really rewarding.

Of course, most chess players are just ordinary folk. Still, chess acts as a sort of universal language, and if you travel, you are sure to find chessplayers almost everywhere you go. Chess is so popular that almost all nations are members of FIDE, the World Chess Federation.

The list of the strongest chess playing nations might surprise you. The map on the next page shows where the top chess powers are (from darkest to lightest), based on the average ranking of each nation's top ten players. You should be aware that "nation" has a different meaning for FIDE than for the United Nations. Each of the countries that makes up Great Britain, for example, is a distinct chess territory with one vote. Chess long ago recognized the status of the Palestinian people by granting them their own federation. FIDE has tried to find a way to let all the people of the world participate in chess, even when they have to dance around a few political landmines.

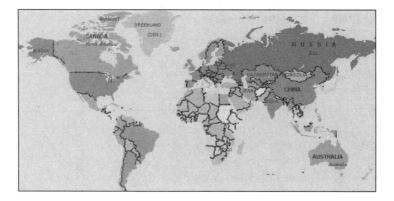

If any man plays at chess and should quarrel in consequence and kill his opponent, such homicide shall be accounted involuntary and not voluntary ... for he employeth himself in a lawful work.
– *Pope Innocent III* (c. 1200)

Where Did Chess Come From?

The Master said: Are there not games played on boards? To play them would surely be better than doing nothing at all.
— *Confucius*

The origins of the game of chess remain a fiercely debated topic. Just about everyone agrees that an early form of the game was in use back in the sixth century, and likely before. It is generally believed that modern chess is derived from an ancient game known as *chaturanga*, a game played in India with four equal armies on a four-sided board. Archaeological evidence of what might be pieces used in a related game back in the second century was uncovered in 1972. Over thirty years later, the origin of chess remains shrouded in history.

I believe that the game of chess received a modified version of the old name, *chaturanga*, to become *chatrang*. That name can still be found in such far-flung places as Cambodia, where it remains the word used for the game. As a linguist, I find the evidence for an Indian origin of the game quite persuasive, but some people, primarily in China, argue that the game was invented there. I'm not going to get into an academic debate here. There are many books on the history of chess, and lots of resources on the World Wide Web. So, in what follows, keep in mind that I'm presenting the views of scholars and authorities I happen to agree with.

Assuming that chess had its origins in Buddhist northern India sometime in the first half of the first millennium, the spread of the game throughout the world can be traced. One plausible scenario is that the earliest expansion went along with the spread of Buddhism, especially into Southeast Asia. Chess may have been present in China as early as the sixth century.

As you can tell, I've been walking on eggshells while laying out a scenario for the early history of the game. People who are into chess history can be quite obsessive and very defensive about their theories, not unusual in a community of researchers. I have not done any formal research into this tricky area, except to do some linguistic reconstruction. If you are interested in passionate arguments and claims of definitive analysis, you can join the pursuit of truth yourself, or just follow the action in journal articles, books, and on the Internet. One interesting site to check out is "On the Origins of Chess" (**www.mynetcologne.de/~nc-jostenge/index.htm**).

As the world entered the ninth century, still quite a long time ago, things became a lot clearer and less controversial. A flourishing city played an important and even critical role in the expansion of chess: Baghdad.

Baghdad in the Eighth Century

By the end of the eighth century, chess had spread westward and had become popular in the Muslim world. Nowhere was chess more prominent than in the ancient city of Baghdad, especially during the reign of Caliph Harun al-Rashid. The caliph was one of the most important figures in the early history of chess, but of course, he is better known as that fellow who had to listen to those thousand and one tales told by Scheherazade.

He not only played chess, he also encouraged those around him to play chess, too—even the slaves! It is said that he spent ten thousand gold pieces purchasing a slave with high chess skills, who earned her lover's freedom by defeating al-Rashid in a match. Another legend claims that the caliph sent a magnificent chess set to Emperor Charlemagne, who was also reputed to play the game. Scholars don't think much of these legends, but one of Scheherazade's tales seems more plausible—until you consider that the rules of chess had not yet been modified to include powerful queens. They did, however, include promotion of a pawn to a new Vizier—the name of the piece at the time—with more limited powers than the modern queen.

From Burton's Translation of the Arabian Nights Tales

She [Tawaddud] said, It hath reached me, O auspicious King, that when the damsel was playing chess with the expert in presence of the Commander of the Faithful, Harun al-Rashid, whatever move he made was speedily countered by her, till she beat him and he found himself checkmated. Quoth he, "I did but lead thee on, that thou mightest think thyself skilful: but set up again, and thou shalt see."

So they placed the pieces a second time, when he said in himself, "Open thine eyes or she will beat thee." And he fell to moving no piece, save after calculation, and ceased not to play, till she said, "Thy King is dead!--Checkmate." When he saw this he was confounded at her quickness and understanding; but she laughed and said, "O professor, I will make a wager with thee on this third game. I will give thee the queen and the right-hand castle and the left-hand knight; if thou beat me, take my clothes, and if I beat thee, I will take thy clothes." Replied he, "I agree to this;" and they replaced the pieces, she removing queen, castle, and knight.

Then said she, "Move, O master." So he moved, saying to himself, "I cannot but beat her, with such odds," and planned a combination; but, behold, she moved on, little by little, till she made one of her pawns a queen and pushing up to him pawns and other pieces, to take off his attention, set one in his way and tempted him to take it. Accordingly, he took it and she said to him, "The measure is meted and the loads equally balanced. Eat till thou are over-full; naught shall be thy ruin, O son of Adam, save thy greed. Knowest thou not that I did but tempt thee, that I might finesse thee? See: this is check-mate!" adding, "So doff off thy clothes." Quoth he, "Leave me my bag-trousers, so Allah repay thee;" and he swore by Allah that he would contend with none, so long as Tawaddud abode in the realm of Baghdad.

In any case, it seems to be solid historical truth that Harun al-Rashid was a great popularizer of the game of chess. It is reported that anyone who showed considerable skill at chess was most welcome in his court. He is known to have been absolutely lavish with his rewards to those who demonstrated their skills and managed to impress him. The details may be the stuff of legend, but the caliph is a historical figure who is enshrined in the annals of chess history.

♟ ♛ THE ORIGIN OF THE WORD "CHESS"

The English word *chess* ultimately derives from the Persian word *Shah*, which means "king." *Checkmate* comes from *shah mat*, meaning "death to the king." You can still find the Persian influence in many languages; for example, "chess" in German is *schach*, in Russian it is *shakhmaty*, and in Finnish it is *sakki*.

In the Far East, the ancient Sanskrit term *chaturang* is generally considered the ancestor of the word "chess." For example, in Farsi, a modern Persian language, the word for "chess" is *shatrandzh*. Furthermore, "chess" is *shatranj* in Hindi, *shatrang* Arabic, *catur* in Indonesian, *chatrang* in Khmer (Cambodian), and *sataranji* in Swahili.

The Conquest of Europe

Near the end of the first millennium, chess infiltrated into Europe. Within a century, it had become commonplace in the courts of Europe, as well as in the Muslim lands. We know that chess came in from Persia because important chess words, including "chess" itself, are easily established as borrowings. Accounts of the time period include references to chess in a number of countries.

Chess remained an exceedingly popular game in Europe throughout the second millennium. It was enjoyed by commoners and royalty alike. The list of kings and queens known to have played chess reads like a Who's Who of European history. Even if a royal didn't actually play the game, it is probable that that fact would never be admitted in public.

Of course, the Europeans had to place the game of chess in their own cultural context, and quickly replaced the Arabic pieces and names with their own. The Shah became the *king*, the vizier became the *queen*, the elephant turned into a *bishop*, the horse became a *knight*, the chariot became a *rook*, and a foot soldier became a *pawn*.

After a few hundred years, a few rules were changed and the game became a bit more sophisticated. To speed things up in the early stages of the game, double moves were introduced. The pawn was granted a special privilege of moving forward two squares on its first turn, rather than the single square advance it is usually restricted to. Castling, a double move of the king and rook, helped get the monarch out of the center quickly and to a safer home closer to the corner of the board. These were relatively minor modifications, but it is difficult for a modern player to conceive of playing under the old rules. Almost all of the modern understanding of how to play the first stage of the game radically depends on those innovations.

At the end of the Renaissance, the rules settled down to the form we have today. Chess was still a casual activity, and matches between individuals were the only form of competition. It wasn't until the mid-nineteenth century that international chess tournaments established themselves, starting with the great London International Tournament of 1851.

Globalization

By the middle of the nineteenth century, chess had spread to most of the globe. The game traveled with soldiers, sailors, and explorers. Long journeys were made a little less tedious because the game entertained travelers. Chess quickly became common among not only the wealthiest and most influential persons, but the commoners, too. Chess found a special home in the coffeehouses of Europe. Indeed, for a long time, these coffeehouses were the most important places in the chess world.

International chess competitions became commonplace in the latter half of the nineteenth century and continued to grow in popularity except when interrupted by global conflicts. The rise of communism was accompanied by a huge wave of interest in chess, because the mind sport was made a priority in most communist nations. The Soviet Union quickly came to dominate the international chess scene.

The Soviets took control of the World Championship just after World War II. From 1950 until 1972, all of the World Champions came from the Soviet Union, as did all their title match opponents. That all changed when Bobby Fischer shocked the world by winning the title from Boris Spassky in convincing fashion in their 1972 match in Reykjavík, Iceland. That match was closely followed throughout the world, and it looked as though Fischer might hold onto the title for a long time.

However, Fischer was stripped of the title in 1975 when he declined to defend the title under rules and regulations set forth by the World Chess Federation. The Soviet idol Anatoly Karpov then claimed the title for a decade. Meanwhile, the Soviet players continued to dominate both individual and team competitions.

During the same time period, FIDE did a magnificent job establishing chess federations in many countries throughout the world. What had previously been a sport of primarily wealthy, developed nations became a truly global activity and was established as the second most popular competitive activity.

Chess is played non-stop at Waikiki's Prince Kuhio Beach, in Hawaii

Before Bobby Fischer's success, professional chess existed mostly in the communist world. Prizes in competition were simply pathetic. The prize fund for the World Championship was just a few hundred dollars, because the communist countries controlled the conditions under which the competition was played. Once the game became a worldwide sport, prize funds increased rapidly, and sponsorship came flooding into the game.

Although for some time the countries of the former Soviet Union continued to produce the best players, the globalization of the game, combined with a great deal of emigration from those countries, leveled the playing field. Players from the former Soviet Union can be found all over the world. In fact, all six players on the 2004 United States men's Olympiad squad were born in Russia.

Today's Top Players

Here is a list of some of the world's best players and the national federations they represent.

Alexei Shirov	**Spain**
Etienne Bacrot	**France**
Garry Kasparov	**Russia**
Judit Polgar	**Hungary**
Michael Adams	**England**
Peter Leko	**Hungary**
Ruslan Ponomariov	**Ukraine**
Vassily Ivanchuk	**Ukraine**
Veselin Topalov	**Bulgaria**
Viswanathan Anand	**India**
Vladimir Kramnik	**Russia**

CHAPTER 2
Rankings for All

Chess offers a clear way to measure your skill against the skills of all the other players in the world. A mathematically sophisticated ranking system is applied not just at the international level, but also by national federations, local chess clubs, and even casual online chess sites. The rating system is not perfect, of course, but it is sufficiently accurate that bookmakers in Las Vegas refuse to offer odds on chess competitions because they feel that the rating system makes it too easy to predict overall results. The ranking system was developed by Dr. Arpad Emre Elo in 1959 and adopted by FIDE in 1970. It has now been applied to some other sports and activities, including, amusingly enough, professional wrestling.

You might want to jump right into the rating pool when you begin playing chess, but you will be better off if you wait until you have some experience in the game, and at least know the basics of the opening, middlegame, and endgame. You can get unofficial ratings by playing online or perhaps at a local chess club. You would be wise to get an unofficial rating of 1000 or higher before starting official rated play. Otherwise, you might start with a very low rating and have to slowly and painfully climb your way up.

When you feel you are ready to get a rating, you can do so by joining the United States Chess Federation (**www.uschess.org**) and participating in one of its sanctioned tournaments. There are many tournaments held each weekend all over the country. Your rating will depend on how well you do.

All of the major ranking lists use some form of the rating system devised by Elo. The scale is roughly zero to 3000, though no one has achieved anything near 2900 yet on the official lists. The numbers are translated to more meaningful terms in the chart below.

Rating	Class	Number of Players on 2005 FIDE List
2800	World Champion or top contender	1
2700	World Championship candidate	16
2600	World Class Grandmasters	116
2500	International Grandmaster	526
2400	International Master	1826
2300	FIDE Master	5025
2200	National Master	12048
2000	Candidate Master	31646
1800	Advanced Tournament Player	6627
1600	Tournament Player	—
1400	Club Player	—
1200	Casual Player	—
Less than 1200	Beginner	—

In 2005, a minimum rating of 1800 was required to be on the FIDE list.

These designations should not be confused with official titles. The requirements for international titles are more complicated. We'll get to those in just a bit. The small number of rated players between 1800 and 2000 is due to the fact that such ratings were only introduced in 2004; a minimum of 2000 had previously been required. At one time there was a separate rating floor for women, but this was done away with. The new system allows all players to qualify for a published international ranking if they can reach the 1400s.

Modern tournament software does all the rating and qualifying norm calculations for you, which is a good thing, because, surprisingly, chess players are not always good at arithmetic!

Ratings play an important role in tournament competition, as the rating not only determines the pairings, or matches between two players, but is also used for prize qualification.

The most widely accepted ratings are those of the World Chess Federation (FIDE). These are published twice a year and are available on the Internet. This list has grown to almost fifty thousand players, even though it is restricted to those who have earned a relatively high ranking. FIDE is lowering the minimum rating requirement, so that soon all players at the tournament level or higher will be included. Updated lists are always available online at **www.fide.com**. The FIDE player rating database information is publicly available and allows us to paint a nice picture of the modern chess scene.

There is also a monthly rating list known as the professional world ratings. This list uses some different formulas that are said to be an improvement on the traditional method. Garry Kasparov dominates this list as well as the FIDE list. The ranking lists of the United States Chess Federation, which includes even absolute beginners, is officially updated every other month.

Online chess clubs also offer ratings, but these are not as reliable. The relationship between online ratings and the official USCF and FIDE ratings can be large. The Internet Chess Club keeps track of how they compare by a survey. As I write, ICC ratings are an average of 115 points higher than the same player's USCF rating, and about 75 points higher than FIDE. Still, almost one-third of the users have lower ICC ratings than USCF ratings.

Calculating ratings for historical players remains somewhat controversial. The classic question arises: were the great players of the past as strong as modern, full-time professionals with computer research facilities and an enormous amount of literature to draw on? Jeff Sonas has done a tremendous job applying his own theories at **www.chessmetrics.com**. I have done work along very different lines at Chess City (**www.chesscity.com**). The inventor of the rating system, Dr. Arpad Elo, tackled the problem in his book, *The Rating of Chessplayers Past and Present*. Nathan Divinsky and Raymond Keene tried to determine the best players of all time in their book, *Warriors of the Mind*. Though there is a small hobby industry in determining them, historical ratings are not generally accepted because they can vary so greatly, depending on the system used.

International Titles

Skilled chess players can earn titles awarded by the World Chess Federation. The highest title is that of *International Grandmaster*, or just *Grandmaster*, as no other Grandmaster titles are generally recognized. You'll often see the abbreviation GM attached to a chess player's name. That means that he holds the title of Grandmaster, not that he has been somehow genetically modified.

The Grandmaster title is earned by holding a very high rating and performing exceptionally well in official competition. There are presently almost one thousand Grandmasters, from over seventy-five countries.

The rank below Grandmaster is that of *International Master*, abbreviated IM. This title is earned in the same fashion as that of Grandmaster, but the requirements are far less stringent. There are more than 2500 International Masters from over one hundred countries.

Earning an international rating of 2300 or higher is reported by the title of *FIDE Master*, or FM, which signifies that the player is recognized as a master by FIDE, but has not reached the rank of International Master. There are over four thousand FIDE Masters.

FIDE also bestows special titles for women, though most female players prefer to compete for the general titles.

National chess federations and even local organizations often award their own chess master titles, but these are not generally recognized outside those domains. As for the title of World Champion, the World Chess Federation offers many different championship titles, including separate events for boys and girls in the under 10, under 12, under 14, under 18, and under 20 age groups, as well as a senior title for those over the age of 60. As far as the overall World Champion is concerned, that is a much messier picture.

World Championship

The whole idea of an organized World Championship for an individual sport originated with Wilhelm Steinitz, who not only set up the first World Championship, but managed to win it. Steinitz had already been acknowledged by many as the strongest player in the world, but he wanted to make it official. So, after emigrating to the United States, Steinitz took on the number one contender, Johannes Zukertort, in a match for the grand sum of $2000. Of course, when the match took place in 1886, that was an enormous sum of money.

There is very little debate about the first thirteen world chess champions. After that it gets a bit messy because the World Chess Federation, which controlled the title from 1948 until the early 1990s, drastically changed the format for determining the champion. Traditionally, the check and champions have been chosen in a head-to-head match with the number one contender. That contender had to earn the right to be the challenger by winning a sequence of events, some of which were tournaments and others were matches of as many as sixteen games.

FIDE was interested in speeding up the traditional three-year cycle. The goal was to have annual World Championship events. This did not allow time for many qualifying events, so they turned the whole thing into a big knockout tournament, where initially the matches were just two games, and luck suddenly became a huge factor. When matches are tied, the players break the tie by playing rapid games where hand speed could be as important as chess skill. As a result, few people outside of FIDE officials consider the winner a legitimate World Champion belonging to the grand legacy of the game.

The thirteenth World Champion, Garry Kasparov, who won the title in 1985, found FIDE's changes to be unacceptable, as did much of the chess world. So, in 1993 he set up a title match under the auspices of his own chess organization. He defended his title twice, but then lost it in 2000 to Vladimir Kramnik. Meanwhile, FIDE had been anointing its own champion, the winner of their knockout tournament, which included a brief match between the two finalists.

The situation has since become even murkier. Kasparov, who retired in 2005, remains the top-ranked player in the world by rating, but has no champion title. FIDE recognizes the winner of their last championship event, Veselin Topalov, as champion. Most of the world recognizes Topalov as the "FIDE champion" or "FIDE World Champion." An attempt to unify the championship titles has been underway for some time. All of the major parties signed a document known as the Prague agreement, setting out terms under which the best players could sort the matter out over the chessboard. Although that plan never came to fruition, FIDE eventually got Kramnik and Topalov to agree to a unification match in the fall of 2006.

In 2004, Kramnik squeaked through and defended his title. Negotiations for the other match did not prove successful, and as this book is being written, no resolution is in sight. Kasparov issued a statement in January 2005, giving up on the title reunification quest. In March, after winning the Linares Supertournament, he retired from professional competition, having given up on the possibility of an acceptable resolution to the World Championship situation and other problems with professional chess. He plans to devote his future to reforming Russian politics, but will continue to play in exhibitions and just for fun.

Sadly, Kramnik has joined Kasparov on the sidelines, due to illness, and cancelled his appearances for early 2006. Time will tell if he recovers his form after dealing with the medical problems.

Developments in the ongoing saga of the world chess championship come quickly, and if you are interested in this subject I suggest that you turn to the Internet to catch up. There are many accounts of how the whole mess came about, and the sketch I've given above is from the perspective of one who has worked in various capacities in most of the championship events organized by Kasparov, though I have also worked with FIDE and strongly support FIDE as the legitimate world body for chess in general.

The World Champions

These are the generally recognized world chess champions, as well as the official FIDE champions since the 1993 split.

1. Wilhelm Steinitz, 1886–1894
2. Emanuel Lasker, 1894–1921
3. Jose Raul Capablanca, 1921–1927
4. Alexander Alekhine, 1927–1935, 1937–1946
5. Max Euwe, 1935–1937
6. Mikhail Botvinnik, 1948–1957, 1958–1960, 1961–1963
7. Vasily Smyslov, 1957–1958
8. Mikhail Tal, 1960–1961
9. Tigran Petrosian, 1963–1969
10. Boris Spassky, 1969–1972
11. Bobby Fischer, 1972–1975
12. Anatoly Karpov, 1975–1985
13. Garry Kasparov, 1985–2000
14. Vladimir Kramnik, 2000–?

FIDE World Champions

1. Anatoly Karpov, 1993–99
2. Alexander Khalifman, 1999–2000
3. Viswanathan Anand, 2000–2002
4. Ruslan Ponomariov, 2002–2004
5. Rustam Kasimdzhanov, 2004
6. Veselin Topalov, 2005

The Chess Olympics

Although the World Championship has been organized by various groups and individuals, the Chess Olympiad has been organized by FIDE since the earliest days of the organization. Beginning in 1927 in London, there have been thirty-four official Chess Olympiads so far.

For some time, the World Chess Federation lobbied to get chess into the Olympics, even if only as a demonstration sport. Though Bridge slipped in, things didn't work out for chess. According to the International Olympic Committee,

FIDE remains the officially recognized organization for chess. But while things looked promising for a while, the IOC now seems determined to reduce, not expand, the games. However, the flirtation with Olympic chess did give rise to one thing—FIDE introduced drug-testing rules. But more on that later.

All of the World Champions from 1927 onward have played in the Olympiad, usually with spectacular results. The reigning champion, Jose Capablanca, had played in the initial 1927 Olympiad event. Alekhine had a perfect 9-0 score in the 1930 event. He hadn't been allowed to play in 1928, however, because at that time, professionals were banned from the games. The rule, originally inspired by the Olympic Games, was quickly dropped. It took a long time for the Olympics to come to the same conclusion about the eligibility of professionals!

Over five thousand players have taken part in the Olympiad, representing 185 countries, some of which don't even exist anymore. The most famous celebrity participant was Marcel Duchamp, the famous artist and one of the best players from France. The youngest participant—an eleven year old—and the oldest—a seventy-nine year old—both hailed from the Virgin Islands.

Hungary, Poland, and the United States were the initial winners. Russia, formerly the Soviet Union, dominated the event for most of the rest of the century. Success in chess seemed to be part of the political game plan of the Soviet Union. Chess was encouraged in most communist countries. The Americans won the Olympiad in 1976, but only because the Soviets refused to play in Israel, where the event was held. The Hungarians were the surprise winners in 1978. In 2004, Ukraine, formerly part of the Soviet Union, took top honors.

The Top Teams in 2004

The honor roll from the 2004 Olympiad in Calvia, Spain included some surprising countries. Cuba has had a proud chess tradition, going back to World Champion Jose Capablanca. India, where the game was born, has a tremendous team, led by Viswanathan Anand, who was ranked #2 in the world. The Dutch also have a long tradition of chess, and claim the fifth World Champion, Max Euwe. Israel has for some time been a team made up mostly of immigrants from the former Soviet Union, but then 2004's U.S. squad were all born there, too. Spain is led by Latvian-born Alexei Shirov, one of the world's best players, and Bulgaria benefits from Veselin Topalov.

The top teams of 2004 were: Ukraine, Russia, Armenia, United States, Israel, India, Cuba, Netherlands, Bulgaria, and Spain.

As with many international sporting competitions, politics have often had an effect on the competition. In 1939, Palestine was awarded a tie against Germany, who did not play them. Countries at war do not have to play each other, and when the event was held in a round robin system, the scheduled match was declared drawn. In 1972, Albania withdrew, rather than play Israel. The Palestinian Liberation Organization, which represented Palestine, did not have to play Israel, and most Arab countries are not paired against Israel. In a 1988 side event, which is an individual competition where players have to play very quickly, there was an incident where, according to the posted pairings, an Arab and Israeli player actually sat down to play each other. Team officials had to intervene to stop the contest.

However, Olympiads have brought together chess players from nations with bad relations. For the most part, they have been a wonderful example of people getting along. An interesting bit of diplomacy took place in the dining hall during the 1980 Olympiad in Malta. The organizers had not prepared for vegetarians, and were puzzled by the requests from various sorts of vegetarians. At the time, I ate mostly vegetarian food, along with fish, cheese, and eggs. Still, when the staff approached me—I was one of the arbiters of the event—and asked what to do for them, I half-jokingly laid out an ambitious menu and suggested that those who ate eggs could do with some nice omelets.

The inventive staff came up with excellent food, much better than the airline-food trays everyone else got. The Muslim and Israeli players were among the first to declare themselves "semi-vegetarians," and wound up spending some time together. Soon other players caught on, and there was a rush for the "veggie" food. It quickly ran out, and before long, the staff, like their airline counterparts, found that it was possible to serve up uninteresting food to suit any diet!

Olympiads remain extraordinarily popular. They involve thousands of players and hundreds of trainers, staff, chess officials, and hangers-on. Perhaps that's why the Olympic Games decided not to bring in chess; it would have been a huge logistical problem!

Show Me the Money!

Chess is a major sport with appropriately major prizes. The classical World Championship matches featured millions of dollars in prizes, with just two contestants. The prize fund for one open tournament in 2005 had half a million dollars at stake, with a great deal of it reserved for less skilled players. The HB Global Chess Challenge held in Minneapolis in May 2005 set new records for the amount of money at stake. Even a beginner could win thousands of dollars! In fact, it would be possible to work your way up through the rating list, picking up big prize money along the way!

One of the most surprising elements of the American chess scene, which is quite different from that in the rest of the world, is that the majority of prize fund money is reserved for players in specific ranking groups. Especially in America, where tournaments are often organized so that they create a profit for those in charge, huge prizes are awarded to players who barely know how to move the pieces. Prizes reserved for players rated under 1200, for example, can involve thousands of dollars! These prizes can be so large that some people deliberately lose games to keep their rating low, just to qualify for the prize. This makes it more difficult for the honest player to win them. Many sane people wonder why such large prizes are awarded, but the math is simple. Offer up one big prize, get lots of people to ante up entry fees of hundreds of dollars, and pocket the profit. That's the way some organizers look at it. In Europe, these "class prizes" are modest sums, intended to cover the cost of attendance, and nothing more.

The HB Global Chess Challenge Prize Fund

Open Section (anyone can play)	
1st place	$50,000
2nd place	$25,000
3rd place	$12,500
4th place	$7,000
5th place	$3,500
6th place	$2,000
7th–20th	$1,000 each
21st–50th	$500 each

Prize for ratings of 2300–2449	
1st place	$20,000
2nd place	$10,000
3rd place	$5,000

Prize for ratings of Under 2300	
1st place	$20,000
2nd place	$10,000
3rd place	$5,000

Separate sections for players rated under 2200, under 2000, under 1800, and under 1600	
1st place	$20,000
2nd place	$10,000
3rd place	$5,000
4th place	$2,500
5th place	$1,500
6th place	$1,000
7th–20th	$500 each
21st–50th	$300 each

Section for players rated under 1400	
1st place	$12,000
2nd place	$6,000
3rd place	$3,000
4th place	$2,000
5th place	$1,500
6th place	$1,000
7th–20th	$500 each
21st–50th	$300 each

Top Under 1200	
1st place	$10,000
2nd place	$5,000
3rd place	$3,000
4th place	$2,000
5th place	$1,000

Top Under 1000	
1st place	$4,000
2nd place	$2,000
3rd place	$1,000
4th place	$1,000
5th place	$1,000

Section for players who are unrated	
1st place	$2,000
2nd place	$1,000
3rd place	$600
4th place	$500
5th place	$400
6th-10th	$200 each

Betting on Chess

Throughout the history of chess, players and spectators have placed wagers on games. It was only recently, however, that wagering on chess grew into a small industry. It is now possible to wager on who will win a competition and on all of the individual games in a major competition. In fact, unlike any other sport I know of, you can even bet on a game while it is in progress. The odds can change from move to move. This fascinating aspect of the game was introduced by a company called Betsson (**www.betsson.com**). Chris Duncan of Betsson explains how it works below.

> Bets on chess use decimal odds. Decimal odds are the European way of quoting odds, but they are very easy to understand. For example, if you bet on Russia to win the Olympiad at 1.6 for 100 euros, then you would receive back 160 euros, making a net win of 60 euros. USA was quoted at odds of 40; if you bet 100 euros then you would receive back 4,000 euros, giving you a net win of 3,900 euros.
>
> For an individual game, you might back Kasparov at 2.10 for 100 euros. This means that you want Kasparov to win the game. Your total return, if Kasparov wins, is 210 euros (odds x stake). If Kasparov does not win (draw or the loss) your loss is 100 euros (your stake).
>
> You can place orders, which means that you can enter your wishes into a bet exchange's database, and when a matching offer has been found, your bet will be made. For example, you want to bet on Kasparov winning, but the only odds on offer are 1.5 and 1.45. You want at least 1.6 before you consider betting 100 euros on Kasparov. Therefore you enter your wanted odds and the stake you want to bet into the database, and if someone later has "laid" an offer which matches your wish, the bet will be carried out. The system works the same way for those who want to "lay" bets (act like bookmakers). You can, for instance, lay Kasparov at 1.65 for 100 euros, which is the same as saying, " I don't think Kasparov will win this match. I offer odds of 1.65 on Kasparov, and I accept a maximum of 100 euros on this match. If Kasparov wins, I will pay you 1.65 times your stake, If Kasparov loses or draws, I will win your stake."
>
> If you are used to the usual way of betting, it may take some time to get accustomed to this form of betting, where you can choose and present your own odds. However, once you're familiar with this form of betting, you will most definitively like it a lot. There is even a very good chance that you will make easier money this way, than by ordinary betting, where you need to fight the profit margins of the professional bookmakers.

Of course, Mr. Duncan, himself a formidable chess master, would like you to believe that it is easy to win money by betting on chess, as he works for a betting company. Wagering on chess involves the same degree of risk as any other bet. You might think that the ability to wager while the game is in progress means that you will have an advantage if you are able to properly evaluate the state of play. You have to remember, however, that almost everyone has access to powerful computer programs that are capable, in the majority of cases, of accurately evaluating the position. So if you offer odds that differ greatly from the computer evaluations and the online live commentary, your offer is likely to hold great risk. On the other hand, if you are offering a bet that conforms to the predictions of the computers and analysts, who in their right mind is going to accept it?

Still, many chess fans greatly enjoy placing small wagers on chess. As for the legality of such bets, that obviously depends on where you live and what laws apply to that jurisdiction. In a few short years, betting on chess has grown into a sizable industry, so it seems that the reluctance of bookmakers in Las Vegas to open their cash registers to the chess market may have been misguided. The chess ranking system doesn't predict most of the results, all it can do is predict the overall odds. Remember, a chess game will either be won or drawn. The rating system might predict that in a contest between two players, one of them is likely to win 70 percent of the time. However, this does not predict the result of any individual game.

Buckle, Lord Lyttleton, and many eminent in chess, were strongly in favor of the customary small stake, and I have seen dignitaries of the Church, and spotless amateurs, pocket their shillings with as much gusto as the poor and much abused professional. It is a kind of voucher to mark the score.
—*Henry Bird* (on wagering)

Sometimes a strong player gives a weak player some advantage at the start of a game, to make things more interesting. Rarely does one start without one's queen, but that's what Norwood Potter did in his nineteenth century game. And after just six moves, he announced checkmate.

To really make life tough when giving odds, you can stipulate that checkmate must be delivered with a specific piece. This is called a "capped" piece. All the opponent has to do is capture that piece, at any price, and you lose.

CHAPTER 3
A Few Chess FAQs

Even people who have never played chess already have opinions on what the game is all about. Though some of their ideas might be right on target, not all people who play chess fit the stereotypical image of a pocket-protector-wearing nerd. Below are a few frequently asked questions about chess and the best answers I can give you.

Do You Have to be a Nerd to Play Chess?

No. Carmen Kass, a supermodel, was elected president of the Estonian Chess Federation in 2004.

Grandmaster Alexandra Kosteniuk

Arnold Schwarzenegger

Furthermore, there is even a professional wrestler, Randall Black, who goes by the chess-themed name of "Rook Black." And no matter what your political views are, you have to admit that Arnold Schwarzenegger is not a nerd, and he's a fanatical chess player.

Does Chess Really Improve Academic Test Results?

Yes. Chess has, in fact, been demonstrated to significantly increase scores on standard tests. There have been many academic studies proving the point, but really it's just common sense. Chess teaches essential problem solving skills that can be put to use in a variety of testing environments. In some ways, chess is just a big multiple-choice test—you might have up to fifty possible moves in the game at any point, but only a few moves will be worthy of serious consideration.

The academic community in the United States has finally recognized the value of chess, and it is now part of the curriculum in many elementary schools. In some schools, chess is available to all students, while other schools sometimes restrict chess programs to students who have demonstrated high intelligence and good study habits.

"I have six children, and I've always encouraged all of them to play chess. I think it helps to sort the brain out."
—*Sting*

Do You Have to Be a Genius to Be a Chess Master?

This remains a matter of some dispute, although some work has been offered to show that in order to become a strong chess master, a respectably high IQ of 130 or so is needed. IQ tests given to top chess players have shown exceptionally high marks, especially Bobby Fischer. His IQ has been reported to be higher than 180.

In my experience, the skills required to play chess well can be acquired by anyone. To reach the level of mastery, however, an above average intelligence does seem to be required. Then again, if you sit around with top chess players and discuss politics, you might find yourself reconsidering the link between chess and intelligence.

Since the tests given to measure IQ focus on pattern recognition and recall, it does seem fairly obvious that a strong chessplayer will do well on such tests. However, even the best chess players make some very stupid moves at times—a generally humbling experience which prevents all but a few from getting carried away by their egos.

Can You Play Chess in Jail?

Yes. Chess is permitted in most prisons. Many authorities consider chess a very useful activity because it keeps people out of trouble. Indeed, I've often referred to chess as the world's greatest waste of time. Chess can absorb hours and hours of a person's time—not just during games, but also when solving puzzles, reading books, and so on. Logically, then, chess is a very natural activity for people who are incarcerated.

This game serves marvelously for those who find themselves shut up in prisons, wherein they are continually inventing some honest pastime which may mitigate and sweeten that odious tediousness.
— *Giovanni Battista Verci*

While many prisoners are given access to chess sets, chess books can be a bit more troublesome. Some prisons refuse to allow chess books to be sent to prisoners and to be placed in a prison library because they are afraid that the cryptic chess moves might contain some sort of secret gang code. If you don't believe me, just take a look at the rejection notice below. Let me point out, however, that after the publisher forwarded me the message, I got in touch with the Oregon Governor's office, and they very quickly cleared up the matter and changed the policy. They immediately agreed that this policy was just plain stupid. Still, there are other places that limit chess books for the same foolish reason.

```
                                                                          3G 38A
                          OREGON DEPARTMENT OF CORRECTIONS
                                                              Facility Address
    Date: 4-13-01            PUBLICATION VIOLATION NOTICE      Snake River Correctional Institution
                                                              777 Stanton Blvd.
    Staff: DH                                                 Ontario, OR 97914

    Mail addressed to Inmate: Robert Madison    SID number: 13353605  is in violation of the
    Department of Corrections (DOC) Rule governing Mail (Inmate).  The material has been rejected because it:

    ☐  Contains sexually explicit material
    ☒  Contains material that threatens or is detrimental to the security, safety, health, good order, or discipline of the facility, inmate
       rehabilitation or facilitates criminal activity
    ☐  Contains credit or deferred billing transactions
    ☐  Contains items prohibited from receipt by mail
    ☐  Contains unauthorized business transactions
    ☐  Contains mail that is subject to outgoing mail restriction
    ☐  Contains other material that the Department deems to be detrimental to legitimate penological objectives

    Cite specific article(s) and page number(s) or material(s), considered objectionable:
    Contains Code Throughout

                   ADMINISTRATIVE REVIEW ONLY FOR WRITTEN OR PICTORIAL CONTENT
    Pursuant to OAR 291-131-0050, a sender or intended inmate recipient who has received a publication violation notice may obtain
    independent review of the rejection of a publication by writing to the Functional Unit Manager or designee at the above address, and
    requesting an administrative review.  A request for an administrative review must be in writing and received within 30 days of the date
    of the notice, and should specify the reason(s) why the rejection should not be sustained.

    To Sender: Cardoza Publications   Rejected   Standard Chess
    Address: 132 Hastings St          Publication: Openings
             Brooklyn NY 11235

    Distribution: White-Sender/Yellow-Mailroom/Pink-Intended Inmate Recipient        CD 618c (12/98)
```

Can Chess Be Dangerous?

Yes...sort of. Chess is such an absorbing activity that it can be dangerous if it is allowed to block out everything else that is going on in the world. For example, it's just possible that the United States of America succeeded in the Battle of Trenton because the British general was given information about George Washington's pending attack, but was too busy playing chess and didn't look at the message, instead just put it in his pocket. He then completely forgot about it, and when his body was dragged back from the unsuccessful battle, the note was still sitting there, presumably unread.

The devil was a great fool to use so many machinations to make poor Job lose patience. He had only to engage him at a game of chess.
—Gilles Menage

Many claims have been made for chess, sometimes suggesting that it can be a sort of miracle solution for personal problems, substance abuse, and getting into college. It is true that playing chess helps develop the ability to make decisions quickly, even under pressure. However, you have to realize that just being able to make a decision quickly doesn't mean that you will always make good decisions. Indeed, playing too much chess and spending too little time socializing usually leads to awkward situations in real life.

A Question for You

I've answered a few of your burning questions about chess. Now it's time for you to answer a question and test your memory and observation skills in the process. Don't worry, the answer is printed below. Which of the following films does not have a chess scene?

2001: A Space Odyssey	*Play it Again, Sam*
Austin Powers	*Play Misty for Me*
Bad Company	*Rambo III*
Bedazzled	*Rocky VI*
Black Hawk Down	*Searching for Bobby Fischer*
Blade	*Shaft 2000*
Blade Runner	*Stalag 17*
Blazing Saddles	*Star Wars*
Casablanca	*Superfly*
Casper	*Superman II*
Dawn of the Dead	*The Front*
George of the Jungle	*The Luzhin Defense*
Harry Potter and the Sorcerer's Stone	*The Seventh Seal*
Hercules in New York	*The Three Musketeers*
Independence Day	*Twins*
Natural Born Killers	*X-Men*

Answer: Bedazzled. The film originally had a chess scene, but it ended up on the cutting room floor. However, the scene was included in the director's cut DVD.

For a big listing and photos of films that feature chess, visit the "Chess in the Cinema" Web site (**www.skgiessen.de/movies**).

CHAPTER 4
Ready to Play

The Basic Rules of the Game

Chess is a game where two players alternate taking turns moving their forces around a chessboard. The goal of the game is to place the opponent's king in a position where it cannot escape capture. On each turn, a player may move one piece according to the rules that govern the movement of that piece. There are six different types of pieces, which I'll discuss in more detail later.

Chess sets and boards can be made of almost any conceivable material. Chess sets are considered an art form, and some are valued at millions of dollars. On the other hand, cheap plastic chess sets can be purchased for just a couple of dollars. If you don't have one handy, you can even improvise your own chess set. For example, you can create chess sets using different coins to represent the pieces. Or, as I was sometimes known to do during boring periods in school classes, you can actually just draw the pieces on scraps of paper and draw a chessboard on a larger piece of paper.

Let's look at the chessboard first, and then move on to consider the roles of the chess pieces.

47

The Battlefield

The game is played on a checkered, square board, made up of sixty-four alternating light and dark squares. The light and dark squares are arranged in rows of eight groups of eight. The vertical lines, those running up and down the board, are called **files**, while the horizontal lines, those running back and forth, are called **ranks**. Notice that the files are lettered, from a through h, while the ranks are numbered, from 1 through 8. The diagonal lines, which run along a 45 degree angle and contain squares of only one color, are simply called **diagonals**. Note also that a light square is always in the lower right hand corner as a player sits at the board. It always amuses chess players to see how often television and film directors get this simple setup wrong!

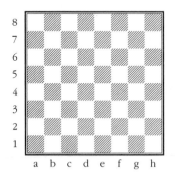

Because many boards do not have black and white squares—most are brown or green and beige, and some even have red squares—chess players refer to them as **light** and **dark**. Along those lines, the pieces are referred to as **Black** and **White**, regardless of their actual color. Just remember to be color blind, and you won't go wrong.

The Forces

Each side gets an assortment of pieces and pawns. There are only six different chess pieces, each represented by a different symbol. We will use these symbols throughout the book.

♔	White King		♚	Black King
♕	White Queen		♛	Black Queen
♖	White Rook		♜	Black Rook
♗	White Bishop		♝	Black Bishop
♘	White Knight		♞	Black Knight
♙	White Pawn		♟	Black Pawn

The pieces can vary greatly in design. In most competitive chess, the standard chess set is based on a nineteenth-century design by the English player Howard Staunton.

One team is called White, the other Black. White has the privilege of moving first. In the early days, the first move could be made by either White or Black, but during the nineteenth century it became standard practice for White to move first. In tournament play, the colors are assigned. In casual play, informal arrangements are used. For example, a player may place a white pawn in one hand and a black pawn in the other, and holds them behind his back. The other player chooses a hand, and plays with the color of the pawn enclosed in the hand he chose. Chess sets do not have to have white and black pieces; any two colors will do. In this case, the lighter color is considered White.

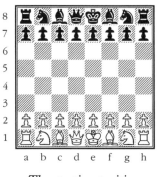

The starting position.

The pieces and pawns are set up as shown in the diagram, with a light square in the closest right hand corner. The king and queen sit in the middle, flanked by bishops, knights, and finally rooks, with pawns in front, facing the enemy. Another way to make sure you have the king and queen on the right squares is to think of the king as the emperor, since he starts on the e-file, and the queen as the dame, since she sets up on the d-file. This will only work if you set the board up correctly, with the first and second ranks for White and the seventh and eighth ranks for Black.

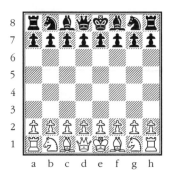

The game begins when the player controlling the White pieces makes a move, and continues with Black and White alternating moves until one player traps the opposing king, which is called **checkmate**. The game could also end with one of several possible draws, where neither side wins. We'll examine those later.

The King

The king is the most important chess piece. Each side has just one king, and the game ends when either king is about to be captured. In the game of chess, a king cannot be killed or captured. Chess is an ancient game, and for most of its existence, kings in the real world were very important and powerful people. Clearly, in a civilized world they would not be subject to such mistreatment as would remove them from the chessboard.

The goal of the game is to place the enemy king in such a position that he cannot avoid capture, were capturing the king actually legal. When a situation is reached where a king would be subject to capture on the next turn no matter what happened, we would have a situation known as **checkmate**. We'll get to that a bit later on, but for now, let's see what you can do with kings.

The king is represented by an icon which resembles a crown, often with a little cross at the top. This small Christian decoration has caused some controversy in the game, as some societies frown upon importing books with Christian symbols. On one of my earliest trips to Russia, which was then under Communist rule, I was shocked that at the border, the customs officials seemed very concerned about the chess books that I had purchased in Germany. Since these were books printed in communist East Germany, I surely didn't expect any problem bringing them with me into the Soviet Union. However, a customs official kept pointing at the kings on the chess diagrams in the book. Amazingly, I had stumbled on one of the rare Russian male adults who didn't actually play chess and knew nothing about it. As I stood there in confusion, a carrier walked over, took one look at the book, and enriched my vocabulary of Russian vulgarities by giving the customs official a real dressing down.

In the diagram below, a White king sits on the square e1.

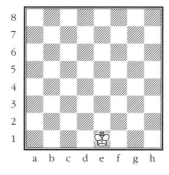

The king on his home square.

King's have the power to raise low things and to abase high things, and make of their subjects like men at chess; a pawn to take a bishop or a knight, and to cry up or down any of their subjects.
—*King James the First of England*

Although the king is the most important chess piece, he is also the least powerful. The king is limited to a single step; he may only move to an adjacent square. If he stands in the center of the board, where there is the most room to maneuver, he is nevertheless limited to just eight potential moves. These are represented by stars in the diagram below.

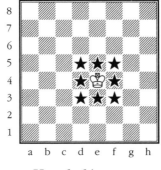

How the king moves.

The king has one additional move, an innovation introduced a bit over five hundred years ago, when the pace of the game was felt to be a little too slow. Under certain circumstances, the king may move two squares horizontally in the maneuver known as **castling**. Castling is the primary method used to get the king to safety early in the game. You'll learn all about castling later.

Who are the Kings of Chess?

The official world champions may be considered the "kings of chess," but there are a number of other players who are thought of as unofficial world champions because they dominated chess before the creation of the world chess championship in 1886. Of course, there is much discussion and debate concerning their worthiness to wear the crown.

If we want to assign a title to each of the best players in recorded chess history, we can make a reasonable start in the latter part of the eighteenth century. In France, Francois-André Philidor was the best player in the world, and he was also a famous composer! At the end of the century, he passed the baton to his countryman, Alexandre Deschapelles, who passed it on to yet another Frenchman, Louis Charles de la Bourdonnais, who was clearly the best player of the third and fourth decades of the nineteenth century.

Then the focus moved from France to England, where Howard Staunton, designer of the standard chess pieces in use today, dominated the growing field of talented players. Strangely, just when London was introducing formal international chess tournaments, a German player, Adolf Anderssen, became the dominant player. He was eclipsed by an American, Paul Morphy, at the end of the 1850s, but with Morphy's abrupt retirement, Anderssen was again considered the world's best player until the era of official World Champions began with Steinitz in 1866.

The international credentials for the unofficial titles do not favor a single chess nation. Included are representatives from France, England, Germany, and the United States.

Who are the Chess-Playing Kings?

The royal game has had royal fans ever since the beginning. It has been considered the sort of activity that kings, queens, and other nobles could and should enjoy. Of course, one had to be careful when playing against a member of the royal family. Sometimes it was unwise to win, as the consequences could be grave indeed. For example, when William the Conqueror lost a game, he smashed the chessboard over his opponent's head.

Almost all of the most famous monarchs played some chess. Napoleon, Charlemagne, Louis XIV and Louis XV, and even one of the kings of the Incas, who managed to pick up the game while Europeans were destroying his country. The Aztec king Montezuma also played. It should come as no surprise that the tsars of Russia, where the game has been an institution ever since it arrived, were also enthusiastic players. Many of the kings of England also spent a great deal of time at the chessboard, and Henry VIII even employed someone just to make chess pieces.

The Rook

The rook moves in a straight line and may move as far as the edge of the board along either a rank or a file, provided that no friendly or enemy piece is in the way. As with all chess pieces (except for the knight), the rook cannot jump over any pieces, but can capture an enemy piece, of course.

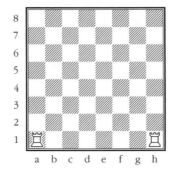

The rooks in their starting positions.

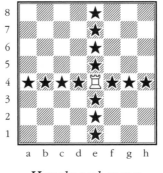

How the rook moves.

The Bishop

The bishop is similar to the rook except that it moves only along diagonals. Therefore, it is restricted to only moving to squares of the same color as the square it is occupying. This is a very significant difference, meaning that the bishop is generally less powerful than the rook, which can find its way to any square on the board.

Bishops in their starting positions.

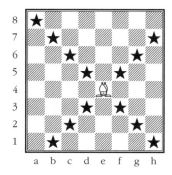

How the bishop moves.

The Queen

The queen is the most powerful chess piece. She combines the power of the rook and the bishop, and can move as far as the edge of the board along any rank, file, or diagonal. It wasn't always this way, however. In the early days of chess, the queen was simply a *vizier*, or "wise man." However, once the piece was elevated to the status of the queen, she became a powerful destructive force.

The queen in her starting position.

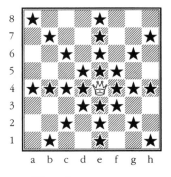

How the queen moves.

Who are the Queens of Chess?

Female chess players have been around since the time of Scheherazade, though by the nineteenth century, chess had become an activity played mostly by men in private clubs, where women were generally not allowed. During the first half of the twentieth century, women's chess was completely separate from men's. Women had their own competitions, and starting in 1927, there was even an official women's World Championship. The very first championship, organized by the World Chess Federation, was won by the Russian player Vera Menchik, who dominated women's chess for two decades, defending her title successfully each time. In the second half of the century, women's chess reached its peak in what was then the Soviet Republic of Georgia. Georgian players kept control of the women's title through the 1980s. Then everything changed.

The Polgar sisters were raised from birth to be chess players. All three achieved major international success, with the oldest, Susan, seizing the women's world title. But the real star was the youngest, Judit, who shocked the world when she earned the title of International Grandmaster at the age of fifteen.

In 1988, the three sisters played together as the Hungarian team in the world chess Olympiad, and they managed to defeat the powerful women's team from the Soviet Union in a massive upset. Susan and Judit remain at the top of women's chess, and Judit is ranked as a top-ten player in the world, regardless of gender. The Polgar sisters are truly the queens of the chess world.

Who are the Chess-Playing Queens?

It isn't all that surprising that royal women often spent time playing chess. After all, while their husbands were all making war, holding endless meetings, or just watching their backs, the women had a lot of free time on their hands.

As chess spread westward, it was quickly taken up by royals, both queens and kings alike. There are plenty of examples of chess playing queens in eleventh-century Spain, for example. Back then, the queen on the chessboard had not acquired great powers; it was still the Persian wise man. That soon changed.

As chess worked its way northward, the queen began to develop. In the twelfth century, Eleanor of Aquitaine, who held titles of queen of France and queen of England, among others, was known to be very supportive of the game. She had probably learned it as a child, as it was included in the basic education of royals at the time.

Playing chess became part of the lives of many queens, and sometimes the game plays a role in how they are remembered. For example, in paintings dating from the fourteenth century, we see Queen Arabel of Germany teaching chess and receiving religious instruction in return.

In Russia, it took quite a while for the idea of the queen on the chessboard to catch on, and even as late as the seventeenth century, most chess sets had the old vizier instead of the new queen. However, once Catherine the Great ascended to the throne, things changed very quickly!

The Knight

The move of the knight is a bit complicated and often causes some trouble for beginners. To start with, the knight is the only chess piece that can jump over another piece, whether friend or enemy. In addition, the shape of the move is a bit strange. The knight moves in the shape of the letter L. It moves two squares along either a rank or a file, then shifts one square in an intersecting direction. If it has traveled two squares on the rank, it moves vertically to an adjacent square on the file. If the two-square move is along a file, then it shifts horizontally to an adjacent square on the rank. A knight always moves to a square the opposite color of the one from which it departs.

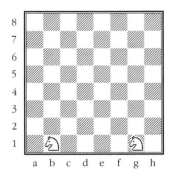

The knights in starting position.

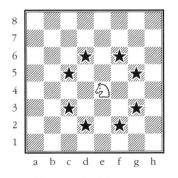

How the knight moves.

I like to sneak up on people. Let them think one thing about me, then
surprise them with something different. That's just like the knight. The
knight sits there, and you don't think he can get you because of the way
he moves.
—*LaVar Arrington,* Washington Redskins

The peculiar moves of the knight make it much more sensitive to location on the
chessboard. The knight pictured above is quite happy, with access to the maximum
number of squares it can reach: eight. However, if the knight is stuck in one of the
four corners of the board, it is miserable.

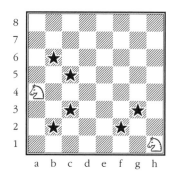

Knight in the corner and on the edge.

In the corner, the knight has just two possible moves. On the side of the board,
it has four. So, knights are generally most effective when they are out in the open,
somewhere near the center of the board.

The Pawn

The pawns are the infantry of the chessboard, but they have great potential for
advancement.

I'd rather have a pawn than a finger.
—*Grandmaster Reuben Fine,* World Championship contender

It all depends: which pawn and which finger?
—*Grandmaster Roman Dzindzichashvili*

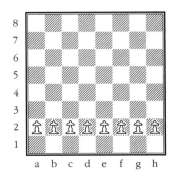

Pawns on their home squares.

MOVING PAWNS

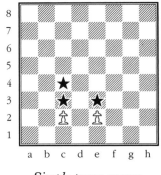

Simple pawn moves.

The pawn is unlike the pieces. Its basic move is one square forward along a file except for the first time it is moved, when it can move one *or* two squares. However, once it has moved, it may only move one square at a time.

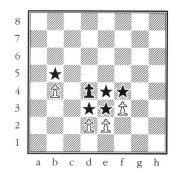

The above diagram shows more pawn moves. For example, the pawn on the f3 square has already moved one space, so the next time it moves, it may only go one square forward to f4, not two squares.

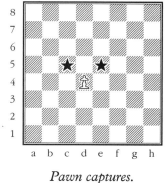

Pawn captures.

Unlike all the other pieces, the pawn captures in a different way from its normal move. In order to make a capture with a pawn, it must move one square forward along a diagonal—never a file.

Pawn is blocked.

When a pawn or some other enemy piece stands immediately in front of your pawn, you can't capture it and you can't move forward. Your pawn is stopped and has no legal moves.

EN PASSANT CAPTURE

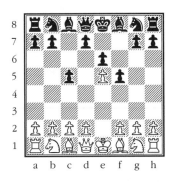

En passant is a French phrase meaning "in passing." It is a special pawn move for a special situation. When a pawn moves forward two squares instead of one on his first turn, he can be captured by an enemy pawn as if he had moved forward only one square. Of course, the enemy pawn must be in position to capture him if he had moved forward only one square.

As with castling, this move has extra restrictions. An en passant capture is only possible as a direct answer to the enemy pawn move. Wait a move, and you lose the right. Also, it is restricted to a pawn capturing another pawn. White can only capture en passant with a pawn that stands on the fifth rank, while Black can only make the move with a pawn on the fourth rank.

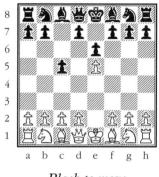

Black to move

This is a possible starting position for the en passant maneuver. Note the position of the pawns on the central files.

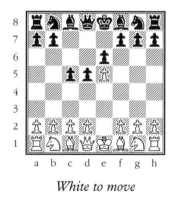

White to move

White captures the pawn on d5 as if it were on d6.

The Black pawn has not yet been removed from the board.

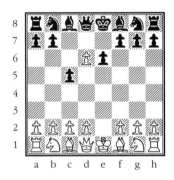

The en passant capture completed.

Promotion

Pawns are also unique because when each pawn reaches the end of the file, which is the eighth rank for a White pawn or the first rank for a Black pawn, the little guy promotes. This means he turns into one of the pieces—either a knight, a bishop, a rook, or a queen. He cannot promote to a king or refuse to promote.

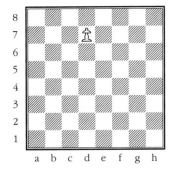

Pawn on the 7th rank.

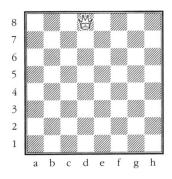

Pawn has promoted to a new queen.

The pawns are about to be promoted.

"The Eighth Square at last!" she cried. ... "Oh, how glad I am to get here! And what *is* this on my head?"
—*Lewis Carroll, Through the Looking Glass (And What Alice Found There)*

The White pawn has promoted to a new queen. The Black pawn can now capture the rook and promote to a queen as well.

The Black pawn has promoted after capturing the rook.

For pawns to promote, it doesn't matter which pieces are still on the board or which are captured. This makes it quite possible to have four or five—or even more—queens on the board at the same time!

A GAME THAT NEVER WAS

ALEXANDER ALEKHINE VS. GRIGORIYEV
ALLEGEDLY PLAYED IN MOSCOW, IN 1915

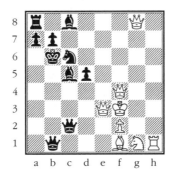

Position just after White has created his third queen.

The great chess investigator Tim Krabbé describes how this game is actually a fake. It is an artistic composition by the World Champion. It is, however, a perfectly legal chess position. In fact, Alekhine even created a series of twenty-three moves that could be played to reach the position. The first ten moves were those of a real game he played against Grigoriyev in the Moscow City Championship, a game won by Grigoriyev as Black. In the composed game, White goes on to win, creating a position with five queens on the board at the same time.

It seems that Grigoriyev didn't mind, because he surely was aware of it at least a dozen years later when it was published in a leading Russian chess journal. Perhaps he felt it was such an artistic contribution that chess would be the poorer if he exposed it.

The point of the composition is that White can force a win by moving the rook from h1 to h6. Alekhine, who included this game in his book, *My Best Games of Chess*, goes on to give a beautiful series of moves leading inevitably to victory. This is the final position of the composed game, with the fifth queen the result of the final move, promoting a pawn to a queen on the b1 square.

When you promote a pawn when playing against a computer program, the machine will usually offer you your choice of pieces, because it can create them on the fly. But your regular chess set is not likely to have extra pieces. To promote a pawn to a second or third queen if an extra one isn't available to you, I suggest turning a captured rook upside down or laying a piece on its side. There is always a way!

Summary of Pawn Moves

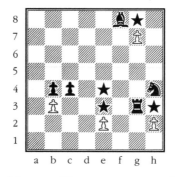

Pawn moves indicated with stars. Three captures are also possible (c4, f8 and g3).

Here is a summary of all legal pawn moves. The White b-pawn can capture the Black c-pawn, but not the Black b-pawn. The White e-pawn can move one or two spaces forward. The White g-pawn can promote to a queen, rook, bishop, or knight by moving forward to the g8 square or by capturing the bishop on the f8 square. The White h-pawn can capture the Black rook on the g3 square or move forward to the h3 square. It cannot capture the Black knight.

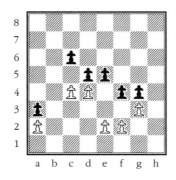

The one rule about pawns that has no exception is that they can never move backward. So you shouldn't advance your pawns prematurely, as you may find that you need them back home for defense!

Check

Before going any further, we need to point out a very important characteristic of the king. He is your most valuable piece and you have to protect him at all costs. If you lose the king, you lose the game. That is why the rules require that whenever your king is attacked by an enemy piece, you must eliminate that threat immediately. When an enemy piece is in a position to capture your king, you are **in check**. In games among beginners, the player who makes the move that places the opponent in check often says so out loud, but this is not considered appropriate in tournaments.

Black's king is in check from the rook.

The object of the game of chess is not to score points or touchdowns; it is to trap the king. He doesn't actually get killed, or captured. When the king is under attack from an enemy piece or pawn, which means that in the next move the king can be captured, it is called **check**. When a king is in check, everything else must be put aside while the king gets out of check. It is not possible to capture the king in chess, so the game ends if he cannot get out of check.

When a king is threatened with capture, he must get out of check. There are three ways to do this.

Check to the king!

The first and usually the best way out of check is to capture the checking piece or pawn. For example, say the Black king is in check along the diagonal from the White queen. To get out of check, Black can **capture** the queen with the knight.

No queen, no check!

Of course, your opponent doesn't usually make things so easy. Let's put the knight back where it came from.

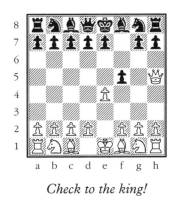

Check to the king!

When you can't capture the checking piece, or if that might be a bad idea for some other reason, your second option is to **block** the check by putting one of your pieces or pawns in the way of the long range checking piece.

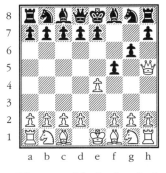

The pawn blocks the check.

This time there is no way to capture White's queen, but Black still has to get out of check. The only way to do that here is to block the diagonal with the g-pawn by moving it one square forward.

No block or capture.

The final method of escape from check is to **run away**. The king may be a slow-moving piece, but he can still get away if the coast is clear. In the diagram above, there is no possible capture or blocking move. The king has to run.

No block or capture.

The king is not in check at f8, so he's safe, for the moment.

Checkmate

If there are no saving moves, it is called **checkmate**. Most of the time, checkmate is shortened to **mate**. So in Australia, they sometimes say, "That's mate, mate!"

There are many checks, but just one checkmate.
—Russian proverb

Black is checkmated!

If you are unable to capture, block, or run away to get out of check, we have a checkmate.

White is checkmated!

In order to play chess intelligently, you have to know what checkmate looks like. Consequently, here are some more checkmates.

Checkmate.

Castling

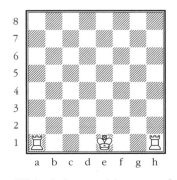

White is in a position to castle.

There is a special move to help your king find safety while waking up a rook called **castling**. It can be done only once a game by each player. It is a double-move in two senses. During one turn, both a rook and the king move, and the king gets to move two squares. Like en passant pawn capture, this special rule was added over five hundred years ago to help speed up the game.

Castling has many restrictions, but first we'll get the basic idea down. In order to castle, the king moves two squares along the home rank in either direction toward a rook, and that rook jumps over the king on the same rank to land on the opposite side on an adjacent square. There can be no pieces of either color on the squares between the king and rook.

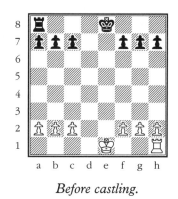

Before castling.

In these two diagrams, White is ready to castle on the king side or **short**, while Black castles queen side or **long**. **Kingside** simply refers to the side of the board where the king starts out, while **queenside** is the other half of the board, where the queen finds itself in the beginning. The next position shows the situation after castling.

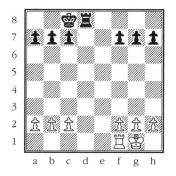

Both sides have completed castling.

You cannot castle if either the king or the rook have already moved from their home squares.

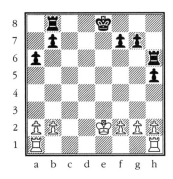

Castling is not allowed in this situation.

Castling is the only time in a game of chess when two friendly pieces can be moved on the same turn. It is also the only time the rook can jump over another piece. No captures can be made, and it must be the first move of the game for both the king and rook. If the king has moved, castling is not allowed. Furthermore, if the rook that the player wants to castle with has moved, there is also no castling, at least with that rook. There are some other rather tricky restrictions to castling, so make sure you know the rule. Even experienced tournament players sometimes castle illegally and allow their opponents to do the same.

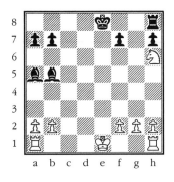

The king can't castle into check, out of check, or through check. The first two restrictions are clear—since you can never move into check, it makes sense that you can't castle into check. Castling is, after all, a move. Castling out of check would be a wonderful resource if you were allowed to do it, but you're not. There are only three ways to get out of check, as you just learned, and castling isn't one of them.

The strangest rule about castling is that you can't castle through check. Even if your king can be perfectly safe on its original square, and the squares between king and rook can be empty, and neither king nor rook has moved, and the king would wind up on a safe square if it could castle, castling is still not allowed if the square the king passes through on its way to safety is covered by an enemy piece or pawn. The following positions illustrate those restrictions having to do with check.

In the first position, White cannot castle because he is in check, while Black cannot castle because the rook has moved.

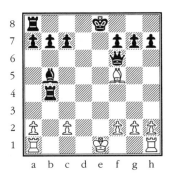

In the second, Black cannot castle into check. White cannot castle through check kingside, but can castle queenside, though the rook and a square it will pass over are controlled by the enemy. The restrictions on castling apply only to the king.

White to move and win a rook.

White wins by castling queenside, putting the enemy king in check while simultaneously attacking the rook at b2.

White wins the rook.

Castling is perfectly legal, since at no time was the White king under attack by the Black rook. However Black responds to the check, White will capture the rook on the next move.

Even the pros get confused!

During the Karpov-Korchnoi match in 1974, Viktor Korchnoi asked the arbiter, Grandmaster O'Kelly, if he could castle if his rook was being attacked. Over two decades later, at a tournament in New York, Korchnoi again wasn't sure whether he could castle. This time, he wasn't sure whether or not he had moved his rook. Of course, this usually isn't a problem because a player just glances at the scoresheet and looks for rook moves. However, Korchnoi's famously illegible scoresheet provided him with no clue as to whether or not he had moved the rook. He asked me, as the arbiter, to let him look at his opponent's scoresheet, but I had to disallow that request, especially since his opponent was in time pressure. After the game I had to remind him that there was no penalty for illegal castling, and therefore if he was in doubt, he should just castle and leave it up to the arbiter or his opponent to protest the move. Of course in that case he would be obliged to move his king, so he'd have to have a safe king move as an alternative!

Quiz on the Rules

Now that I've covered the basics, test your skills by trying to answer the following questions. You'll not only see how much you've learned, you might also start to see things in a new way.

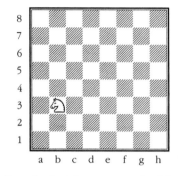

1. Can the knight move to the d4-square?

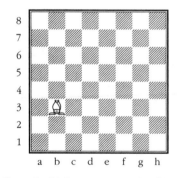

2. Can the bishop move to the d5-square?

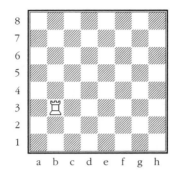

3. Can the rook move to the e6-square?

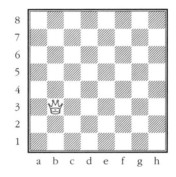

4. Can the queen move to the e6-square?

5. Can White's pawn capture the Black's pawn?

6. *Can the White pawn move two squares to b4?*

7. *Is White's king in check?*

8. *Can White castle, assuming neither the king nor rooks have moved?*

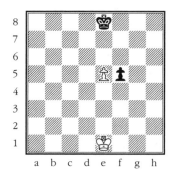

9. Black's pawn has just moved from f6 to f5. Can White capture it?

10. Black's pawn has just moved from f7 to f5. Can White capture it?

1	Yes	6	No
2	Yes	7	No
3	No	8	White can castle queenside, but not kingside.
4	Yes	9	No
5	No	10	Yes, by the en passant rule.

How Much is Each Piece Worth?

Most chess instruction includes a lesson on the value of the pieces. Each different piece is given a numerical value so that you can compare their relative worth. After all, you don't want to exchange a piece of greater value for one of lesser value. However, the real value of a piece depends on many factors, including its location, mobility, and safety. With that in mind, please don't take these numbers as anything but general guidelines. Such values might apply in a situation where the piece is in an ideal position, but that's rarely the case.

The value of the pieces is much more stable in the endgame, when there are very few forces left on the board and pieces can move fairly freely to get to more useful positions. At the very start of the game, the power of each piece in its starting location is predictable. For everything in between, it is important to understand that you need to make adjustments, taking into account other considerations. However, at the same time, you need to keep in mind that as more pieces leave the board, the value of each piece will often return to what it was at the start of the game.

With those very important disclaimers out of the way, let's take a look at the conventional values. You can think of these as purely mathematical numbers, or translate them to dollars and use a financial model. I think it is more fun to play with money, so let's use the financial model.

A pawn is worth a dollar (that's the basic unit we'll use). The minor pieces—the bishop and the knight—are worth three dollars each. A rook is worth a bit more, five dollars. There is no general agreement on what a queen is worth, but it is somewhere in the range of two rooks and can be treated as a ten-dollar piece. As for the king—well, you can't put a price on his head. After all, if you lose the king, you lose the game. So, any tremendously high figure will do. A term used by some chess teachers and students is a "gazillion."

Most introductory materials on chess stick pretty rigorously to those values, and as I've already pointed out, that's not really a good way of thinking about the chess pieces. I really want you to keep in mind how the value of a piece is directly related to its environment. So let's look at a couple of chess positions to illustrate that point.

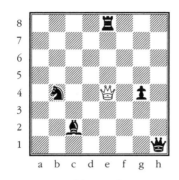

Which piece should the white queen capture?

Here the White queen can capture any of the Black pieces. White should obviously choose to capture the enemy queen at h1, because that is a ten-dollar gain, better than anything else on the menu.

Things aren't usually that simple. In most cases, you'll find that at least some of the targets are defended. If you capture one of those, your queen will be captured and you might have a net loss.

Watch out, there are traps!

I've moved the pieces around a bit, and the result is a position where capturing the queen would just be an even trade. Black's pawn would recapture, and each side would lose ten dollars. The next logical choice is the five-dollar rook at e8, but that rook is guarded by the bishop at a4, so the capture would lose five dollars, giving up the queen for a mere rook. Taking the knight at c2 is even worse, because it is also defended by the bishop. The bishop itself can be captured, and it is not defended. It is just a three-dollar gain, but that's the best. It is worth more than the one-dollar pawn at g4—in any case, that pawn is protected by the enemy queen.

Now that you understand the basic values, below is a chart that shows not just the "all else being equal" cases, but also cases where you gain some sort of advantage that isn't material. These "intangibles" will be discussed later in the book. They include such things as creating weakness in the enemy king position or pawn structure, control of important areas of the board, and placing pieces on particularly useful squares, These are just a few examples, and the skill of determining when exchanges are appropriate is one of the most useful in carrying out your strategies.

	Normally	With benefits
♛	♖ ♖	♖ ♗ ♙
♛	♗ ♗ ♞	♗ ♞ ♙ ♙
♜	♞ ♙ ♙	♞ ♙
♜	♗ ♙ ♙	♗
♞	♙ ♙ ♙	♙ ♙
♗ ♗	♖ ♙	♖ ♗
♗ ♞	♖ ♙	♖ ♙

As you can see, it isn't just a matter of benefits being worth a pawn. That seems to be the case most of the time, but the values expressed in terms of dollars are rounded off to the nearest dollar. A rook and pawn should be worth six dollars, and so should two minor pieces. However, in most circumstances, the two pieces are more useful than a rook and a pawn. Perhaps worth a dime, or even a quarter more. Much depends on where the pawn is and what it is doing!

I know some of this may seem like advanced material, but I think it is very important not to fall into the trap of determining value on a simple point system. Chess wouldn't be so much fun if things were that simple. Still, keep the basic values in mind as a general guideline.

Win, Lose, or Draw?

There are three possible outcomes to a complete game of chess. First, you can win your game and receive a full point. Second, you can lose your game and and receive no points. Third, the game can end in a draw, in which case each player receives half a point. These results can be achieved in a number of ways, not just through checkmate or stalemate. Some of these are only applicable in serious tournament play, while others apply in all chess games.

How to Win (or Lose) the Game

The game is won by the player who has checkmated the opponent's king with a legal move. This immediately ends the game. You also win the game if your opponent **resigns**. Resignation takes place when the opponent either verbally informs the opponent by saying "I resign," or, in formal competition, by stopping the chess clock and signing the scoresheet, indicating the result of the game.

Players generally resign when they see no way of avoiding a loss and know that their opponent is skilled enough to finish off the game without doing something foolish. Even in casual games, it is often more fun to give up on a bad game and try again in a new game. Tipping over the king is traditionally accepted as indicating resignation, but it doesn't technically count. In informal games, though, it can be accepted as a form of resignation. Often the offer of a handshake indicates resignation, though since this gesture also is used to accept the offer of a draw, it is best to also say something to make it clear.

Nobody ever won a game by resigning.
—*Savielly Tartakower*

If you are playing with a chess timer, you can also win the game if your opponent fails to make the required number of moves before time runs out. We'll go into detail on that in the section on time controls.

Death by Slowness

Fritz Saemisch never had much luck with the clock, but as he got older his time troubles became insurmountable. He lost all thirteen of his games by time forfeit at Linköping in 1969.

87

Checkmate Brings Victory

Since checkmate is such an important part of the game, let's take some time to examine a variety of checkmating patterns. Some of these mates have funny and colorful names, while others have more descriptive names.

Back Rank Mate: *A rook moves to the back rank, while the king is trapped by the pawns.*

Anastasia's Mate: *A rook moves to check the king, while the knight covers escape squares.*

Anderssen's Mate: *A rook moves to the back rank corner, protected by a pawn, which in turn is defended by the king.*

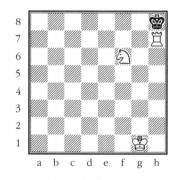

Arabian Mate: *A rook, protected by the knight, moves to check a king in the corner.*

Blackburne's Mate: *One bishop gives check, protected by a knight that covers one flight square, while the other bishop covers the other escape squares.*

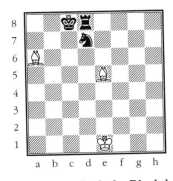

Boden's Mate: *One bishop moves to check the Black king, which is hemmed in by its own pieces and cannot flee because of White's other bishop.*

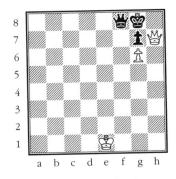

Damiano's Mate: *The queen gives checkmate, protected by the pawn.*

Knight Corner Mate: *Use the knight to give check, while the rook stands guard on the file, and the pawn prevents the king from moving forward.*

Cozio's Mate: *The queen delivers the checkmate, attacking the enemy king while the queen is guarded by its own king.*

Damiano Bishop Mate: *The queen goes directly in front of the king, guarded by the bishop.*

David and Goliath Mate: *A mere pawn checkmates the king, protected by the other pawn. Black's own pieces prevent its escape.*

Double Bishop Mate: *The bishop moves to attack the king along the long diagonal.*

Dovetail Mate: *The queen checkmates the king, protected by the pawn.*

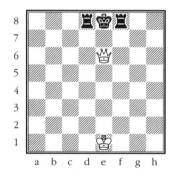

Epaulette Mate: *Move the queen two squares in front of the enemy king, whose flanking rooks prevent any escape.*

Greco's mate: *The queen goes to the right edge of the board.*
The king's escape is cut off by the bishop.

Hook Mate: *The rook slides over to the e-file so that it attacks the king.*
The knight protects it, and the pawn cuts off the remaining flight square.

Corner Mate: *The rook moves to the corner, protected by the bishop.*

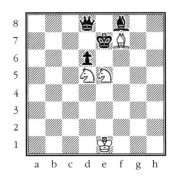

Legall's Mate: *The knight moves into position to check the king. The bishop is guarded by the other knight, and the enemy pieces block the king's escape.*

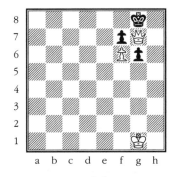

Lolli's Mate: *The pawn can guard the queen on the checkmating square.*

Max Lange's Mate: *The queen moves to checking position next to the king, defended by its bishop.*

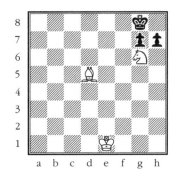

Minor Piece Mate: *White gives check with the bishop, and the knight covers the king's escape squares.*

Morphy's Mate: *The bishop gives check on the long diagonal. The rook and pawn insure that the king cannot escape.*

Reti's Mate: *The bishop goes to the edge of the board, giving check while guarded by the rook.*

Opera Mate: *The rook checkmates on the back rank; it has the bishop as a protector.*

Pillsbury's Mate: *The rook moves over to the g-file to give check to the king, who can't get to the corner because of the bishop.*

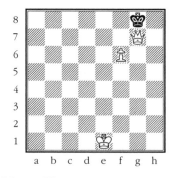

Queen and Pawn Mate: *The pawn acts as a guardian to protect the queen as it checkmates the king.*

Smothered Mate: *The king is surrounded by its own forces, but cannot escape from the knight check.*

Suffocation Mate: *The knight checks at e7, and the bishop covers the escape squares.*

Swallow-Tail Mate: *The queen takes up a position directly in front of the king, defended by the bishop.*

Corridor Mate: *The queen delivers the checkmate on the edge of the board. A rook would do the job just as well.*

Mighty Queen Mate: *The queen moves to the back rank, and checkmates all by itself, since the pawn blocks the king's escape.*

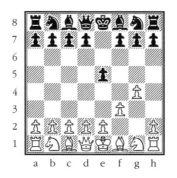

Invitation to Fool's Mate: ***1...Qd8-h4#***

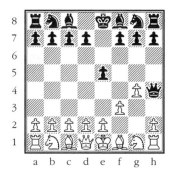

Fool's Mate: *Move the queen from d8 to h4 to achieve Fool's Mate.*
This whole game took just two moves by each side!

Your First Checkmate Strategy

So many checkmates, so little time to learn them all! To get you started, let's take a look at the first checkmate that is learned by almost every chess player.

THE ROOK ROLLER

White applies the rook roller.

The key to most successful checkmating strategies is to drive the enemy king to the edge of the board and then apply a checkmate. In this position, the rooks can accomplish the task by applying a series of checks in a sort of rolling motion.

1.Rb3-b6+   Kf6-e7

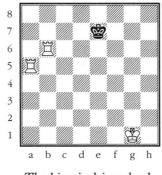

The king is driven back.

The rook moves up from b3 to b6, while the other rook stays in place in order to prevent the king from moving up toward the center of the board. The Black king is forced to retreat. If you have to defend against an attacking rook, the king should generally try to come close to the rook and perhaps attack it from a diagonal square. Here, the king is too far away.

2.Ra5-a7+   Ke7-d8

The king is on the rim.

The roles are reversed, and it is the rook on the a-file that advances to give check, while the one at b6 stays in place so that the king cannot escape the trap.

3.Rb6-b8#

No more room to run.

The king is checkmated on the back rank. Now you know how to apply the rolling rook checkmate! The final position is a corridor mate.

How to Lose Quickly at Chess

You have already seen an example of White's getting checkmated in two moves. Now let's take a look at some other extremely short games of chess. You should certainly try to avoid ever winding up on the losing side of these miniatures.

SUICIDE
1.e2-e4   e7-e5
2.Qd1-h5

Be careful!

This move is often played by beginners because it sets a trap. If Black advances the pawn from g7 to g6, attacking White's queen, then White will capture the pawn at e5 with check and then capture the rook at h8. Black can easily defend against this threat by bringing the knight from b8 to c6, defending the pawn.

2...   **Kf8-e7??**

3.Qh5xe5#

SCHOLAR'S MATE

1.e2-e4   **e7-e5**

2.Qd1-h5   **Nb8-c6**

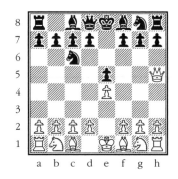

Black wisely defends the pawn at e5 with the knight.

3.Bf1-c4   **Ng8-f6??**

Black overlooks the threat!

Bringing out the knight to attack the queen seems logical, but it overlooks the fatal weakness at f7.

4.Qh5xf7#

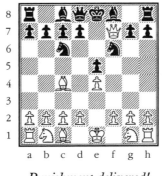

Punishment delivered!

Never forget that when you open up a line to your king, it acts as an invitation to enemy pieces. They may quickly invade your house and cause you much pain. Do not allow it!

How Games are Drawn

The game is drawn when the player to move has no legal move and the king is not in check. The game is said to be in **stalemate**, which immediately ends the game. The game also ends in a draw if both players agree that there really aren't any reasonable prospects for either side to win. It is very important to know the difference between checkmate and stalemate. Since the king is not under attack, the player doesn't lose the game. Instead, the game ends in a draw.

With Wolf I make a draw when *I* want to—not when *he* wants to!
—*Akiba Rubinstein* (when asked why he drew an obviously winning position, according to Fred Reinfeld and Hans Kmoch)

Stalemate!

The position above looks very much like the rolling rook checkmate we examined a bit earlier. If it is White to move, then the checkmate is completed by moving the rook from g6 to g8. However, if it is Black's move, there are no legal moves available, so this is an example of stalemate. White, though just a single move away from checkmate, has to settle for a draw.

The game may be drawn if the identical position is about to appear or has appeared on the chessboard three times or if the last fifty consecutive moves have been made by each player without the movement of any pawn and without the capture of any piece. In competitive play, you summon a tournament official and make the claim. If the moves of the game have not been recorded, there is no way of proving these claims without witnesses. In casual play, these two rules are rarely enforced.

How to Offer a Draw

You may offer a draw whenever it is your turn to move. If the opponent accepts, then the game ends immediately and the result is a draw. If the opponent declines, and makes a move on the chessboard, the game continues. It is impolite to offer your opponent a draw numerous times in the game. If your opponent declines the draw, offer another one only if the position has changed enough to make it even more likely that reasonable play will lead to a draw.

The correct way to offer a draw is to make your move on the chessboard and then say, "I offer you a draw," or just, "Draw?" To accept a draw, you say, "I accept" or something similar. You can also offer a handshake, but that is sometimes used to indicate resignation, so it is better to make your acceptance clear vocally, too.

In the 1970s, there were many complaints that professional players weren't working hard enough. The performance of Bilek at Slupsk in 1979 has often been cited. He drew all ten games, averaging about twelve moves and fewer than ten minutes per game!

As this book is being written, a number of proposals are under consideration to reduce the number of "agreed" draws in short games. American Grandmaster Maurice Ashley has proposed disallowing such draws:

Draws are a natural part of our game, and to play for a win in many positions is stupid if not suicidal. However, the draw offer in a position full of life with mysteries yet to be revealed has got to be the most abused rule in all of chess. I am not even sure you can call this a rule: it is more like a practice that has been regulated, or, in this case, not regulated enough.
—*Maurice Ashley*

Breakfast of Champions

Normally, international chess is played in the afternoon or evening. Chess players tend to detest morning rounds, because that limits their recreational opportunities the night before. However, in many cases the final round of the tournament starts in the morning so that players can leave without having to pay the expense of an extra night at the hotel. Sometimes the morning round is made so that players can catch flights to a relatively nearby tournament starting the next day.

One year at Hastings, the early morning final round included a game between Grandmasters Hort and Larsen that was agreed drawn in just three moves. And on the scoresheet was written: "And off to breakfast!"

Is That Like a Stalemate?

Two future chess masters, your author and Danny Shapiro, once played each other in a scholastic tournament. When I made a move, I forgot to press his clock. Danny had been away from the board, and when he returned, he saw that I could play a winning move, so he offered a draw, not noticing the position had changed. I had to ask him to explain what a draw was! He explained it was like stalemate, but by agreement. I then accepted, because my position was clearly worse. He didn't realize that I had already made my move, because my timer was still running. It was my very first tournament, and I didn't know you could just offer a draw at any time (though it should be done right after making a move). I also wasn't used to playing with chess clocks.

CHAPTER 5
Advanced Rules for Tournament Play

In organized chess competitions, both amateur and professional, there are a number of additional rules that need to be followed. Players are required record their moves on a piece of paper, even though in many cases computerized equipment is tracking the game automatically for display to the public and on the Internet. It is also required that moves be played according to certain time controls. There is a bewildering variety of these time controls, as you'll see a bit further on.

The rules require that each player arrive at the board within 60 minutes of the published starting time of the game. This is not the same as an hour after the game has started, which is what many people believe the rule says. If the game starts late, after a series of typically annoying announcements and speeches by a loquacious tournament director, the deadline may be long past when the flag indicates an hour elapsed on the clock. If the posted starting time is, say, five o'clock in the afternoon, then if the opponent doesn't arrive by six o'clock, the game is forfeit and the late-comer is awarded a big fat bagel (0) on the wall chart, while the player who was present records a win. It doesn't matter if the clock shows a lot of time remaining in the game.

The Arbiter

The officials who enforce rules at chess tournaments are called *arbiters*. They are stationed in the playing hall to insure that all the rules are followed, and they also try to keep the spectators from interfering or making too much noise. As in most sports, they are primarily concerned with infractions of the rules, since out and out cheating is rare.

An arbiter is not usually needed to confirm a checkmate, except at a competition for beginners. However, an arbiter is needed to confirm a draw under the rules regarding repeating the position or the 50-move "no progress" rule.

When a minor rules violation takes place, the arbiter applies a penalty. Penalties open to the arbiter include:

A warning
Increasing the remaining time of the opponent
Reducing the remaining time of the offending player
Declaring the game to be lost
Expulsion from the event

The arbiter has considerable discretion. It is up to the arbiter to decide if some behavior rises to the offence of distracting the opponent. A good arbiter is generally someone who has played chess at the level of international competition and has developed a good sense of how players can be expected to behave.

Many of the arbiters of World Championship matches have been active players with international rankings, and many are Grandmasters. Most of the arbiters with international rankings as players have the respect of the tournament competitors. Arbiters are certified by the World Chess Federation (FIDE), which awards the title *International Arbiter*.

I have the honor of that title, and have officiated at events including the 2000 World Championship match between Garry Kasparov and Vladimir Kramnik. My duties at that event were quite varied. Some of it was quite easy, such as simply checking to make sure that that chess pieces and chess clock were properly set up for the game. It was occasionally a little bit awkward to deal with some of the things such as searching the players and their areas before each game to ensure that no notes or electronic devices were available for their use. The security was similar to that encountered frequently by travelers at airports. We then had to check for electronics with one of those wands used if you set off the metal detector when heading to the gates.

With so much prestige and money at stake, the players are kept under observation at almost all times. During the match, the players even had to be accompanied back to the toilet area. With computer analysis available in so many forms and via so many devices, chess officials have to guard against cheating. Not that anyone expected either of these two players to do any such thing. It is simply that by having all of the safeguards in place, even at the most tense moments of the match when a player may be under great psychological pressure, there was confidence on both sides that nothing inappropriate was going on.

Other World Championship duties includes making sure that spectators do not interfere or conduct analysis in such a way that the players might notice from the stage. In some competitions, the biggest hassle for the arbiter is the photographers. Normally, photography is only allowed during the first few minutes of the game. After that, it is forbidden as a distraction. Nevertheless, when there are a lot of photographers, some can't get the shots they want in the allotted time, and persist in snapping away after the time has expired. Then it is up to the arbiter or security to deal with them.

At one of the chess Olympiads, I often amassed a very nice collection of cameras. They would eventually be returned to the photographers, but the few troublemakers were always punished. Professional chess photographers, and yes there are quite a few, know all the rules and do not cause trouble,. Although still photography is prohibited except at the start of the game, many competitions now have video and web cams operating throughout the game. As long as they are silent, there are no problems for the players or arbiters.

Professional arbiters are rewarded with a nice fee, abundant travel to exotic lands, and have the opportunity to watch great chess being played. Disputes are rare, but when they happen, they are often very messy, can be very bitter, and require considerable skill to get the players to calm down. Most discussion between players and an arbiter will take place offstage, and the majority of disputes are never witnessed by the public. Complaints tend to be made between games, and regard playing conditions more than any specific behavior by a player. However, disputes at the chessboard are especially tricky, because usually there are several games going on at once and a disagreement in one game can bring the whole tournament to a screeching halt.

Boxing as More than a Metaphor

When I was the arbiter of the Edward Lasker Memorial tournament in New York City, one player was upset because he had just lost to an opponent who had drawn most of his games and didn't seem to be making an effort to go all out for a win. The upset player was on the verge of earning a Grandmaster qualification, and couldn't understand why he had been singled out for special attention. The next day, he encountered the opponent in the hallway just after the day's play had begun, and their disagreement got a bit out of hand. Quite a number of punches were thrown, and as the arbiter, it was my job to try the separate the players, so the result is that the majority of the punches landed somewhere on me.

The commotion caused one of the other players to be distracted, and he accidentally played an opening move which was not part of his repertoire. Even though it was only the fourth turn, he realized with horror at what he had done and immediately offered a draw to his opponent. His lower ranked opponent accepted the offer. A minute or two later the boxers had stopped fighting, but many of the players had by that time lost interest in their chess game, and most games were quickly drawn. Though these other players were annoyed with the two fighters, they were even more annoyed the next day, when the two came into the tournament area arm and arm, chatting amicably. By the next day, all the chess players were focused on their games again and the matter was quickly forgotten except to be used as an anecdote making the rounds in the pubs and taverns of the chess world.

With the big egos and substantial amount of money involved, the arbiter has to firmly and fairly enforce the rules, and give no extra benefits to top players. Just as in any sport, superstars must be held to the same standards as everyone else. Of course, in the real world, some arbiters aren't up to that task, feeling intimidated when having to rule against one of the greatest players. Most manage however. Take a look at the photo of renowned arbiter (and poker player) Stewart Reuben. Would you want to start a fight with him?

Don't mess with International Arbiter Stewart Reuben!

American tournaments tend not to use specialized arbiters, but assign the duties to tournament directors. Under rules of the United States Chess Federation, the players are expected to enforce many rules themselves, and there is a greater obligation concerning recording the moves. Some rules are only enforced if the person making the claim has a complete and legible record of the moves. The problems faced in amateur competition are often far more complicated than situations that come up in top professional play, because there are many more rules and the players are often not aware of them.

Touch-Move

This first rule for serious chess games is one you should always observe, even when playing in a class or just for fun. It is known as the *touch-move rule*. Always follow it, because it will build good tournament habits, which can never hurt. Losing a few games now because you refuse to cheat will make you a much better player, not to mention a better person, later.

Touching a piece or pawn during a chess game when it is your turn to move means that you must move that piece or pawn. Once you let go of the piece or pawn, the move is made. If you touch it, you have to move it. If you let it go, the move is made. Furthermore, if you touch your opponent's piece or pawn when it is your move, you must capture it if you can. There is no such thing as a take-back in serious play. Touch-move is strictly enforced. In a casual game with a friend, you might ask to take back an obviously horrible move,. For example if you have an interesting game and then one player accidentally leaves a queen subject to capture, the players might agree to let that move be replaced, just to keep the game interesting.

J'adoube!

There is an exception to the touch-move rule, only available when you wish to adjust a piece on a square where it is perhaps off-center or has fallen down. If you have no intention of moving that piece or pawn, simply say—before you touch it—"J'adoube" or "I adjust," which is what that French term means. This part of the touch-move rule is not, however, meant to save you from making a mistake. If you notice you're making a poor move, or have just made one, you mustn't take it back by saying "J'adoube" or "I adjust."

World Champion Anatoly Karpov and Grandmaster Ulf Anderson adjust their pieces.

One more point about touch-move is that you are not allowed to make an illegal move, such as moving into check or moving a piece incorrectly. If that happens, you must move the touched piece to a legal square. If there are no moves allowed with the piece you touched, you must make a different move. There is no punishment for such a lapse, unless the game is being played at a very fast time control.

Tournament regulations vary, depending on the organization under whose auspices the competition is being carried out. The World Chess Federation has one set of rules, and most nations use those. In the United States, the advanced regulations differ in many respects. Scholastic competitions are often run under a relaxed set of rules. These various rules can be found in rulebooks, including my *Official Rules of Chess*.

Notation

Chess moves are written using a special system known as algebraic chess notation. Tournament players are required to write down moves of the game using an accepted form of chess notation. Most players use a concise, short form of the notation. This book, keeping in mind that most of its readers are beginners, uses the long form, which is much easier to understand.

Each move is described using a system of coordinates. The numbers on the right side of the chessboard describe the horizontal rows, called "ranks." The letters at the bottom indicate the vertical columns, known as "files."

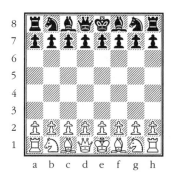

To find the name of a square, you first look at the file, and then find the appropriate rank. In the following diagram, the pawn in the center of the board is at e4.

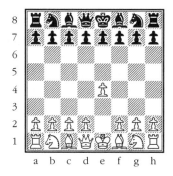

To describe the move that brought the pawn to e4, we indicate both the starting square and landing square, separated buy a hyphen or dash: e2-e4. We put a move number in front of it, so since this is the first move, it's designated 1.e2-e4. That's how we handle normal pawn moves.

If something other than a pawn is involved, we include an abbreviation: for king (K), queen (Q), bishop (B), knight (N) or rook (R). We have to use "N" for knight, since K is already taken by the King, and the king outranks a knight!

White's move to reach the position shown is 1.Ng1-f3. The knight moved from g1 to f3.

So, the system of describing moves is easy enough, but there are a few wrinkles. If the move is a capture, the starting square and landing square are joined by the letter "x." If a knight on f3 captures an enemy pawn at e5, we would write it Nf3xe5, not Nf3-e5.

If the move puts the enemy king in check, it is customary to mark it with a plus sign as a suffix. If a bishop at c4 captures a pawn at f7, placing the enemy king in check, we write Bc4xf7+.

If a pawn advances to the last rank and promotes to another piece, that piece is added after the landing square. If a pawn moved from g7 to g8 and turned into a queen, and the queen places the enemy king in check, we write g7-g8Q+. Checkmate uses a pound sign (#) instead of a plus sign (+).

Castling has special forms too, but for this book, we will just use the word "Castles," and indicate kingside or queenside only if both are possible.

Moves are presented in pairs. So 1.e2-e4, e7-e5 2.Ng1-f3 shows that at the first turn, each player moved the king pawn two squares forward, and then at the second turn, White brought out the knight to f3.

In some places words have been replaced by symbols which, like amulets from a witch's bag, have the power to consume the living spirit of chess. The notorious "!!" can never approximate the human emotions which accompany an "excellent move" or a "great idea".

...Oh, those exclamation points! How they erode the innocent soul of the amateur, removing all hope of allowing him to examine another player's ideas critically!

—*Tigran Petrosian,* World Champion

Here is an example of a complete game, the shortest possible checkmate, known appropriately as "Fool's Mate."

1.g2-g4   e7-e5

2.f2-f4   Qd8-h4!#

If we just want to comment on Black's move, we use an ellipsis (…), for example, Black's checkmating move was 2…Qd8-h4#. The pound/hash sign indicates check-mate.

Notice that above the diagram I have embellished the move with an exclamation mark. In this book we will not use a lot of fancy chess symbols. I will award the exclamation mark to good moves that I want you to pay particular attention to.

You can actually follow all the moves just by moving the piece on the starting square to the indicated landing square. The rest is extra information, included by tradition.

A more concise form of notation is used in most chess books. The short form leaves out the information about the starting square, unless it is necessary. So in the short form, the game would be presented this way: **1.g4 e5 2.f4 Qh4#.** Often the "x" indicating capture is omitted, as is any indication of check or checkmate. Only the information actually needed to figure out the move is included. In this book we'll stick to the long form.

During a tournament game, the players are required to write down their moves on a scoresheet. In American tournaments, the player is technically obliged to write legibly and accurately, though this still doesn't eliminate disputes. Many top players have scoresheets that are impossible to read. You can see an example of the scoresheet of a World Champion:

Let's now take a look at a fragment of one of the most famous games ever played, to see the notation at work.

"THE IMMORTAL GAME"
ADOLPH ANDERSSEN VS. LIONEL KIESERITZKY
CASUAL GAME PLAYED IN LONDON, 1851

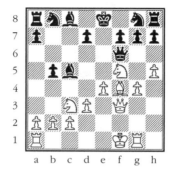

Black has just moved the bishop to c5, attacking White's rook at g1. Black has the advantage of an extra bishop, for which White has only an extra pawn. However, almost all of White's pieces are involved in the game, while Black's pieces are mostly on their original squares. In a position like this, you can't tell who's ahead just by counting pieces!

17.Nc3-d5   Qf6xb2

Anderssen moved the knight to the center of the board, attacking Black's queen. The queen captures White's pawn at b2. Now both of White's rooks are under attack.

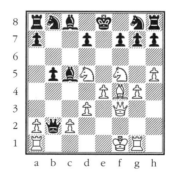

18.Bf4-d6   Bc5xg1

Anderssen moved the bishop from f4 to d6, coming closer to the enemy king. He didn't care that Black could capture the rook at a1 with check. Kieseritzky has a choice of rooks to capture, and decided to take the one at g1 first.   The hungry bishop, which was under attack at c5, captures the rook at g1. Black's advantage has grown to two rooks and a bishop. But six of his pieces still sit on their original squares, and White has a lot of firepower aimed at the king. By the way, if Kieseritzky had captured the bishop at d6 instead, White would have recaptured with the knight from f5, giving check to the king. Black would have been checkmated in just three moves. Kieseritzky should have captured the rook at a1 with check.

♔♕ HELPFUL TIP

In general, capturing pieces while giving check to the king is a good idea, when there is no danger to the capturing piece.

19.e4-e5   Qb2xa1+

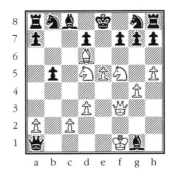

20.Kf1-e2

Kieseritzky gave up, as there was no way of stopping Anderssen from hunting down the king. But the un-played conclusion is an example of great chess art, so let's look at it.

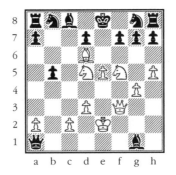

20...   Nb8-a6

Anderssen advanced the pawn from e4 to e5. The purpose of this move was to cut off the communication between Black's queen at a1 and the pawn at g7. The pawn at g7 is attacked by White's knight, and thanks to this move, it no longer has a defender. Black responded by moving the knight to a6 so that the square at c7 is defended. Otherwise, Anderssen would be able to use that square. For example, if Black were to save the pawn at g7 by moving it forward one square, the knight would leap into that square anyway, giving check to the king. The king could not move to f8 or e7 because those squares are guarded by the bishop. So the king would have to shift to d8, and then Anderssen would bring the bishop to e7, check-mating the king.

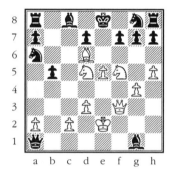

21.Nf5xg7+   Ke8-d8

The knight captured the pawn at g7, at the same time giving check to Black's king. The king had no choice but to slide over to the d8 square.

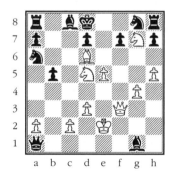

22.Qf3-f6+!   Ng8xf6

Anderssen brilliantly sacrificed his queen on f6, where it was captured by Black's knight from g8. White is down a queen, two rooks, and the bishop for a mere pawn. That doesn't matter, because the game ends on the next turn.

119

23.Bd6-e7#

The bishop gives check at e7, and it is defended by the knight at d5. That knight also covers the escape route at e7. The other knight illuminates the possibility of moving the king to e8. So, Black is in checkmate and Anderssen earned his point.

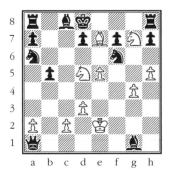

The Scoresheet

The scoresheet is an important part of tournament play. The large chess database of tournament games grows because the recording of games is obligatory at chess tournaments. When the organizers provide scoresheets, they are considered property of the tournament. This affects the rules of the game.

You are generally obliged to keep a legible record of the game in a standard form of algebraic chess notation until you have less than five minutes remaining on your clock in any time control. After each time control is reached, you must fill in any missing moves in your game record. This must be done as soon as time control has been reached. If your opponent has a complete scoresheet, you may ask him (while it is your turn to move) to let you borrow the scoresheet to assist you. The opponent does not have the right to refuse.

When the game ends, it is customary for the players to sign both copies of the scoresheet. It is considered extremely rude, and sometimes against tournament regulations, to fail to sign the scoresheets. When scoresheets include more than one copy, the top copy should be submitted to the tournament arbiters following the procedure of the particular tournament. Failure to turn in a scoresheet may constitute a serious breach of tournament regulations. In American tournaments, the players are also responsible for marking the result of the game on the pairing sheet.

Recently, technology has been introduced to replace written scoresheets with a wireless device that posts the moves directly to the Internet. It is too soon to tell whether this will catch on.

Hiding the Evidence

Some players deliberately hide their scoresheets or make them illegible in hopes that their game, and therefore their opening strategy, will not be published. The plan doesn't work in well-run competitions. The rules state that the scoresheet must be available and visible to the arbiter at all time. Scoresheets are considered the property of the tournament organizers, in most cases. Sometimes they find their way onto auction sites, when they bear the autographs of famous players.

Time Controls

Chess is usually played with a timing device that controls the amount of time each player is allotted. This insures that the game will end within some definite period of time. Chess clocks have been in use for over a century. There are many different time controls, and we'll take a look at a few of them.

The chess clock has two buttons on the top. After you have made your move, you press the button on your side of the clock, using the same hand that moved the piece, which stops your timer and starts your opponent's. After your opponent moves, he or she presses the other button, and your timer resumes the countdown.

A standard digital chess clock

Standard Time Control

The modern standard time control is forty moves in two hours by each player, followed by either all remaining moves in an additional hour each, or another 20 moves in the next hour, followed by all remaining moves in thirty minutes. If a player hasn't made 40 moves by the time the initial 2 hours runs out, that player forfeits the game. When both players have played 40 moves without running out of time, an additional hour is added for each player, and the players then have 60 minutes (plus whatever time they have left over from the first 2 hours) to make it to move 60. After both players have reached move 60, an additional 30 minutes is added, but now the game must be completed before time runs out. Since games can run 100 moves or more, players can get very squeezed for time in this final period.

Things are changing, however, and incremental time controls are increasingly popular. These involve reserving a fixed period of time for each move. In serious chess, this time period is often thirty seconds per move. So the first time control might be forty moves in 100 minutes, with an additional 30 seconds per move. That works out to the same control as forty moves in two hours, except that, under all circumstances, a player must have at least thirty seconds for each of the moves, where without the increment, you can run out of time, altogether. The second time control is twenty moves in fifty minutes, again with thirty seconds per move. The final time control can be all moves in twenty minutes, with thirty seconds per move.

"I was just cogitating ...."

The longest "tank" was the 140-minute contemplation of the 7th move in Trois vs. Santos, at Vigo, 1980. At the time, the standard time control was 40 moves in 150 minutes, so that left Trois with just 10 minutes for 33 moves.

Whatever Happened to Adjournments?

Until rather recently, most professional tournaments and matches allowed for adjourning the game, which means stopping the game at some point and resuming later. Often, games were not finished until a second, third, or even fourth day! At first, players were not allowed to consult with other players, analysts or computers, but eventually the rules were relaxed. In most of the World Championships, especially after World War II, the combatants employed teams of "seconds" to assist with the analysis of adjourned games.

Modern tournaments have done away with adjournments, since the availability of computer analysis would completely remove the human element of the game.

"Sudden Death"

Modern tournament schedules require that each game be finished in a single session. Most games in professional competition are scheduled for either six or seven hours. Normally, the first time control will be something approximating 40 moves in two hours, so a player must average not more than three minutes per move for those first 40 moves. In elite competition, this is usually followed by a time control of 20 moves in one hour, maintaining the three-minute-per-move pace. In other tournaments, players go to sudden death after 40 moves.

In "sudden death," each player is given a fixed amount of time to complete all the remaining moves of the game. If you run out of time, you lose. However, in the digital age, chess clocks have been adapted so that they can add time on each move. This additional time, known as an **increment**, was developed so that the sudden death would not result in a game won by hand-speed rather than chess thinking. Just how much extra time is needed for each move is a highly contentious matter. For the 2000 World Championship, the players instantly agreed to a proposal of just a 10-second addition ---- just enough to ensure that the games would not fall into chaos, but not so much that it could be used for serious thinking. The World Chess Federation prefers a thirty-second increment.

Armageddon

This is a special time control used primarily for tiebreaking. It is almost never used for the first tiebreak, but is resorted to only when other tiebreak methods have failed to break the tie. In this form of chess, White has to win the game, or else the full point goes to Black. In other words, Black has draw odds. In return, White is granted some extra time.

Amateur Time Control

Amateur tournaments tend to be designed to get as many games as possible into a fixed period of time. Often these events are held at schools and other facilities that have a strict limit on when events must end. It is not uncommon for a person to play three or even four games in one day. In general, however, amateur tournaments have two games per day. Time controls vary greatly, but some of the more popular ones are: all moves in two hours, thirty moves in ninety minutes followed by all moves in an hour, and 45 or 50 moves in 2 hours.

World Championship challenger David Bronstein recommends 15 minutes per player per game for casual chess, and thirty minutes for more "creative" games. In the incremental control, friendly games could be 10 minutes per game with a 5-second increment, and 20 minutes with a 10-second increment for more serious encounters.

Blitz Chess

Blitz chess, also known as "rapids," is usually played at a rate of five minutes per player per game. Sometimes the game is even faster, with three-minute chess and "bullet" chess, which allows only one or two seconds per move—especially popular on the internet. Players aren't required to write down the moves; that would be asking too much. There are special regulations for blitz games, often with local variations. So if you play blitz, make sure you and your opponent agree on the rules!

CHAPTER 6
The Opening

A chess game is usually divided into three stages: the opening, the middlegame, and the endgame. In the opening phase of the game, the main concern is to get your forces onto the battlefield, and at the same time, find a safe place for your king. The middlegame is where the fierce battles take place. Then, if neither side is checkmated, the players enter the final stage, or endgame. In the endgame there are not so many pieces on the board; usually just the kings and a few pawns or pieces.

When you set up the pieces to begin a game, they make a pleasing impression visually, but are hardly in battle formation. In the opening phase of the game, you must reposition your forces so that they can attack and defend effectively. There is no boundary that ends the opening. Generally, the opening might be defined differently for each player, depending on how many moves they have planned in advance of the game. For a beginner, sometimes that is just two or three moves. For grandmasters, it might be more than thirty moves for each side!

I might not be faithful with my women, but I'm always faithful with my openings.
—*Grandmaster David Norwood*

 **INCREDIBLE VARIETY**

After the first three moves, there are about 9 million possible positions.

Starting the Game

After many centuries of experience, it should be possible for scholars to determine the best openings strategies, but it is one of the pleasures of chess that this remains an impossible task. The complex interplay of the factors described above makes simplistic statements just seem vain. Nevertheless, we have been able to narrow the candidates.

The first two—and most obvious—candidates are 1.e4 and 1.d4. Each occupies and controls important central territory and allows a bishop to get into the game. The pawn at d4 is protected by the queen, and this fact is sometimes used to argue for 1.d4 being the better opening move.

The starting position

But this is not an important factor, because the goal of either opening is to establish pawns at both squares. Here is the picture after 1.e2-e4.

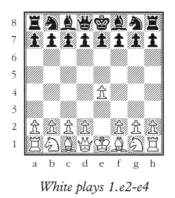

White plays 1.e2-e4

Since the e4-square is slightly more difficult to control, White often seizes control of this square first. Black can try to prevent the White pawn from safely occupying e4 by playing 1...d5 as soon as possible. Of White's first moves, only 1.e2-e4 and 1.c2-c4 discourage this reply, while 1.d2-d4 allows it.

It is generally advisable for beginners and intermediate players to choose a *classical* opening, answering White's first move with a symmetrical choice, for example 1.e4 e5, 1.d4 d5 or 1.c4 c5.

The Names of the Openings

Chess opening strategies usually have names that have become attached to the move sequences for one reason or another. There are over 3000 named chess opening strategies. Historically, chess strategies were often named for the city or region or country where the strategy was popular. So old, established openings bear names like French Defense, English Opening, Scotch Game, Scandinavian Defense, Sicilian Defense, London System, Moscow Variation, and so on. More specific strategies have often been named after players. There are also many openings named for specific chess competitions. Still others have whimsical names. It is hard to tell from the name whether an opening is any good or not. You can see that by having a go at the little quiz below.

STRANGE NAMES

Match the name of the opening with the description

	Name		Description
a	Spanish Inquisition	1	An opening named after a constellation
b	Poisoned Pawn Variation	2	Named for a 19th century player
c	The Dragon	3	Black often moves the queen to a5 very early
d	Frankenstein-Dracula Variation	4	Variation of the Sicilian Defense
e	Fried Liver Attack	5	Named after a World Championship challenger
f	Bogo-Indian	6	A common scholastic opening
g	Czech Defense	7	Main lines of the opening known as the Ruy Lopez
h	The Vulture	8	Complex variation in the Vienna Game
i	Bird Opening	9	An opening where Black gives check at move 2
j	Kangaroo Defense	10	Named after an animal

Correct Answers:

a) 7; b) 4; c) 1; d) 8; e) 6; f) 5; g) 3; h) 10; i) 2; j) 9

Four Keys to Open the Game

I teach my students the four main goals of opening play, so that they can find appropriate moves even when they are in an unfamiliar position. For most beginners, knowing these guidelines is enough to get out of the opening with a respectable position, provided they avoid a few traps. You can use these guidelines to avoid disaster in the opening, while preparing for the main battle ahead.

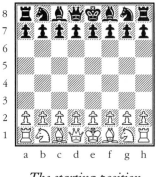

The starting position

Seize the Center

As in many military operations, the first goal is to take control of the center of the battlefield. This advice applies also to most military engagements and to a large number of sporting contests. Control of the center is a powerful tool in establishing the conditions for successful attack.

White occupies the center with pawns

You should send one or two of your pawns to occupy important central squares. Ideally, you will place pawns right in the center of the board at d4 and e4 as White, or d5 and e5 as Black. Naturally, you should also try to prevent your opponent from seizing control of the center. If both sides play well, the situation in the center will be more or less balanced after the first few moves.

Chess is a terrible game. If you have no center, your opponent has a freer position. If you do have a center, then you really have something to worry about!
—*Siegbert Tarrasch*

On the other hand, if you start out by ignoring the center, your opponent will occupy it easily. If you move flank pawns, you jeopardize the safety of your king, since if you castle to that flank, your king will lack cover. Since most games involve castling kingside rather than queenside, advancing the g-pawn two squares forward is considered by many to be the worst possible opening move.

Chess is not skittles!
—*Garry Kasparov,* 13th World Champion (commenting on 1.g4). *Skittles* is a term used to describe informal, non-serious games of chess.

Castling to Safety

Next, you need to turn your attention to your king. The safety of the king is very important early in the game, because until it is safe, it might be attacked by enemy forces. To safeguard your king, you are going to use the special move known as castling. Before you can castle, you need to move out all of the pieces that stand between the king and one of the rooks. It is easiest for the king to castle on the side where there are only two pieces standing between the king and the rook: a bishop and a knight. In the other direction, the queen also would have to be moved.

White is ready to castle

Connecting the Rooks

After you castle, you have to get the rest of your pieces into the game. It is important to consider the role of the rooks. The rooks normally enter the battle from the center of the board, using lines that are opened when some of the central pawns are exchanged. Your third goal is to "connect" the rooks, by making sure that all of the pieces that stand between them are moved out of the way. After castling, of course, the king will already be on the far side of the rooks.

White has castled, and the rooks are connected

Further Adventures of the Rooks

Once your two rooks can "see each other," your fourth and final goal is to move one of the rooks onto a central file, either the d-file or the e-file. You want to use a file that is open for business. A rook can act only as far as it can see, so sitting right behind a pawn is useless, and should be positioned there only when the pawn absolutely requires the protection of the rook.

White has achieved all the goals of the opening

The picture above is only one way of achieving the goals. In practice, of course, your formation will depend on what your opponent does. This is very solid play. Next we will turn to a riskier, but more exciting opening strategy.

The Gambit

A gambit is an opening that involves a sacrifice of material, such as a pawn or piece, to achieve concrete advantages in the position. A gambit is used to establish greater control of the center, a lead in development, a weakness in the enemy king's protection or pawn structure, or to open lines that can be used for an attack. A gambit is not used to win material; such a maneuver would be properly called a pseudo-sacrifice.

The delight in gambits is a sign of chess youth... In very much the same way as the young man, on reaching his manhood years, lays aside the Indian stories and stories of adventure, and turns to the psychological novel, we with maturing experience leave off gambit playing and become interested in the less vivacious but withal more forceful maneuvers of the position player.
—Emanuel Lasker

The word comes from an Italian wrestling term, describing a way of tripping up the opponent. Gambits usually lead to very complicated positions where one slip by the defender may prove fatal.

QUIZ ON THE OPENING

How many opening objectives has White achieved?
1: There is a pawn in the center

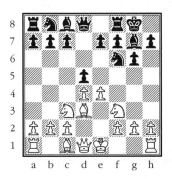

How many opening objectives has Black achieved?
2: Pawn in the center and castling

Black to move. Is this a gambit?
Yes. Black has captured White's d-pawn, and it has not yet been recaptured.

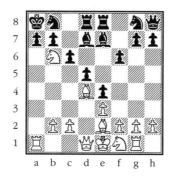

Has Black achieved the four goals?

Yes, but the king is checkmated and the game is over! That shows that you can't be guaranteed absolute safety just by following four simple rules. Chess is a deep and complex game. But this is an extreme, made-up example. Black's pieces are in ridiculous positions, but there are two pawns in the center, rooks are connected and centralized, and queenside castling has taken place. At some point, Black even snatched the a-pawn, perhaps the result of a gambit strategy by White. As for White, not a single one of the four goals has been achieved, but the game is already won!

Still, if you follow the four rules, and don't put your pieces on terrible squares, you'll get good results.

Advanced opening strategies often succeed in spite of not following the guidelines, but there are compensating factors. More often, the goals are achieved, but in a different sequence. There is often a battle in the center of the board, and resources have to be devoted to trying to maintain or gain control of that critical territory.

Some players study openings obsessively, trying to prepare for all the probably replies the opponent might try. This is impossible, because there are simply too many playable strategies. In professional practice, players study openings they expect specific opponents to play, making reference to huge online databases.

For those starting out the game, it is better to concentrate on the middlegame phase, and just learn enough of the opening to get to the middlegame with a respectable position. The school of hard knocks will sometimes teach you painful lessons, but if you learn from experience, you'll soon remove the weeds from your opening garden.

Don't make the mistake of choosing an opening strategy to fit your "style." Until you are a chess master, you don't have a style; you just have a bunch of weaknesses you try to avoid. You'll do better by trying to learn how to play different kinds of positions, and eliminate those weaknesses!

There are only two styles: the losing or the winning one.
—*Vladimir Kramnik,* 14th World Champion

In any case, further opening study is available in the form of hundreds of books offering everything from initial advice to complete opening repertoires containing thousands of moves. Some players love exploring openings; I certainly did when I was young. Others absolutely hate studying openings. At amateur levels, both approaches can succeed, though as competition gets tougher, some basic knowledge of main variations and the ideas behind them is essential.

The opening phase of the game has been studied for a long time, and with the help of computer analysis, so much is known that it is hard to come up with new lines. Since information on any opening strategy is readily available, even from websites, it is hard to surprise serious chess players with new sacrifices early in the game. Once the players are on their own, in positions they have never played before and have not studied, creativity is often rewarded.

CHAPTER 7
The Middlegame

Before the endgame, the gods have placed the middlegame.
—Siegbert Tarrasch

Of course, the mere fact that a position has been previously played and analyzed does not mean that you or your opponent will be familiar with that information. Professional players spend a great deal of time studying all of the data they can so that they can prepare their opening strategy deeply for each encounter. It is not at all unusual to find players working out details of positions that take 30 or more moves to reach. So there isn't really a clear dividing line between the opening and the middlegame, anymore. Informally, the middlegame starts when both players are in territory that is new to them.

Once the middlegame begins, players have to develop strategies to create and exploit weaknesses in the enemy position. These long-term goals are based on such considerations as the safety of the king, and strengths and weaknesses in the pawn structure.

To achieve these goals, players employ tactics. A tactic is a sequence of moves that will lead to some sort of favorable result. There are many different tactics, and you'll meet the most important ones in the next section.

If both armies managed to stave off defeat in the middlegame, eventually enough pieces are removed from the board by capture to bring about an endgame.

When the Fight Is On, Tactics Rule!

A chess tactic is a single move that accomplishes a significant goal. Chess tactics have names, such as fork, pin and skewer. We will examine a collection of tactical devices below.

Chess is 99 percent tactics.
—Richard Teichmann

Although chess is generally associated with strategy, it is really the tactics that decide most games. To be a good chess player, you absolutely must master all of the basic tactics. This is a matter of pattern recognition, so it really comes down to how much time and effort you put into your study of the game.

Strategy requires thought, tactics require observation.
—Max Euwe, 5th World Champion

You have to keep in mind that a chess tactic is not defined by pattern of moves on specific squares. The same tactic can be used in many different positions. Especially when starting out in the game, taking advantage of a tactical possibility is the most common way to win a game. Even grandmasters with decades of experience often fail to spot a tactic in time, and go down to defeat. So when you miss a tactic, as you inevitably will, don't let it get you down.

We're going to look at a few very basic tactics now. Whenever you play a game of chess, try to locate these tactics in every single position. I'll give you some tips on how to do that a little later on.

The Pin

A *pin* in chess is similar to a pin in wrestling. The enemy is put in a position where they cannot move. In chess, it refers to a situation where a piece dare not move, because if it does, a piece behind it will be captured by the same piece that is attacking it.

"The pin is mightier than the sword."
—Fred Reinfeld

The knight is pinned by the bishop

In this position, the knight is *pinned* to the rook. If the knight moves, the bishop will capture the rook. Black can break the pin by moving the rook. If it moves to b5 or d7, it will be in a position to defend the knight.

An absolute pin

This time the knight is pinned to the king, and there is no way to break the pin, since the king would be in check from the rook, and it is illegal to move into check. A pin against the king is known as an *absolute pin*.

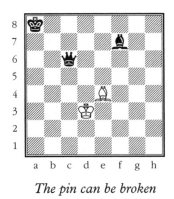

The pin can be broken

The queen is pinned. She cannot move, because the king would be in check. The queen could capture the bishop at e4, but would then be captured by the king. However, the bishop at f7 can move to d5, where it is protected by the queen. This breaks the pin.

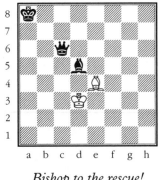

Bishop to the rescue!

The pin is one of the most effective tactics. It can be applied at long range. Pinned pieces are poor defenders and no better as attackers.

A NIGHT AT THE OPERA
PAUL MORPHY VS. COUNT ISOUARD & THE DUKE OF BRUNSWICK
PLAYED IN PARIS, 1858

While most of the audience was following the performance of *The Barber of Seville*, Paul Morphy was busy at a chessboard, facing noble opposition. His opponents, working together, played well enough for a while, but they allowed Morphy to set two deadly pins.

13.Rd1xd7   Rd8xd7

Obviously, Black could not capture with the knight, because it is pinned to the queen by the White bishop at g5. Capturing with the king would have been illegal, because of the bishop on the other side of the board. Naturally, if Black had captured with the queen, the bishop would have captured the queen. So, although Black has increased the advantage in points, with a rook and the knight opposed by White's bishop and two pawns, the two pins are so strong that the fate of the game is already sealed.

14.Rh1-d1   Qe7-e6

After Morphy brought the remaining rook to d1 to increase the pressure at d7, Black took the opportunity to break the pin against the knight by moving the queen forward. This also offers an exchange of queens. Morphy, being behind in material, was certainly not inclined to exchange queens. Instead, he forces his way through to checkmate.

15.Bb5xd7+   Nf6xd7

Black has an extra piece, but Morphy checkmates in two moves. To achieve this objective Morphy sacrifices his queen to get the knight at d7 to move out of the way and allow the rook to reach the checkmating square at d8.

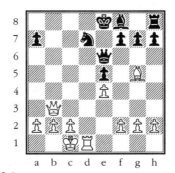

16.Qb3-b8+   Nd7xb8
17.Rd1-d8#

The Fork

You apply a *fork* when your piece attacks more than one enemy piece simultaneously. You can use any of your pieces to create a double attack. Attacking two pieces at once makes it difficult for the opponent to defend, unless the forking piece can be captured. Here are a few examples of how forks can be applied.

Knight forks king and rook

The bishop attacks both rooks

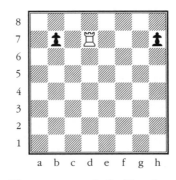

The pawns are forked by the rook

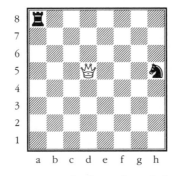

The queen attacks the rook and the knight

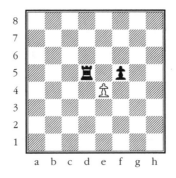

White's pawn has the rook and pawn in a fork

The king forks the knight and rook

Most games of chess include forks. Missing a fork can lead to dreadful consequences at the board, but even world champions sometimes overlook simple forks.

THE SUBTLE QUEEN FORK

LARRY CHRISTIANSEN VS. ANATOLY KARPOV
PLAYED AT WIJK AAN ZEE, 1993

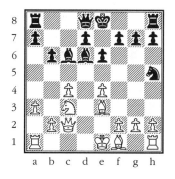

Karpov, as Black, just moved his bishop from its home square to d6, overlooking that the position of that bishop and the knight on the edge of the board gave his American opponent a winning opportunity. Christiansen retreated his queen from c2 to d1, attacking both of those pieces.

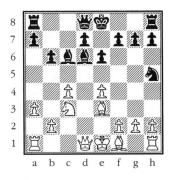

Realizing the horrible consequences of his blunder, Karpov simply resigned. Either the bishop or knight is lost, and against a formidable grandmaster, there was no point in playing on.

X-Ray

An x-ray attack, or skewer, is an inverted pin. The piece in front is attacked, and must get out of the way, allowing the one behind it to be captured. The x-ray can be applied by rook, bishop or queen.

Shish-ka-bob on the 7th rank

The knight and rook are x-rayed

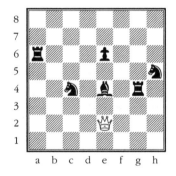

The queen has a triple skewer treat!

X-rays are not as common as forks or pins, but you should never fail to take the opportunity to set one up if the reward is a significant gain of material.

Discovered Attack

The discovered attack is the second most powerful tactic (you'll meet its awesome cousin, the discovered check, next). In a discovered attack, one of your pieces steps aside so that its colleague can attack an enemy piece. The piece you move out of the way is free to go off on a mission of its own, which will likely succeed because the opponent must deal with the discovered attack. In this case, it isn't a matter of one of your pieces attacking two of your enemy's, but rather that two of your pieces independently attack enemy pieces. The discovered attack can be accomplished by any piece, even a lowly pawn.

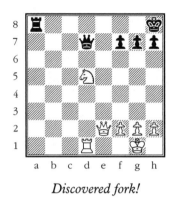

Discovered fork!

In this position the knight can move to b6, attacking Black's queen and rook. At the same time, there is a discovered attack by the rook at d1 against the queen at d7.

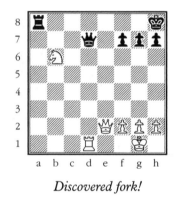

Discovered fork!

In the next example, the bishop is the source of the discovered attack.

Another discovered attack

The discovered attack can be applied in this position in two ways. The rook can move to a4, attacking the knight along the file, or to e7, attacking along the rank.

Discovered Check

The discovered check is even more powerful than a discovered attack, because the enemy king will be forced to deal with the check,, no matter what else may be under attack.

Discovered check is the dive-bomber of the chessboard.
—Grandmaster Reuben Fine

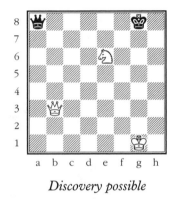

Discovery possible

White moves the knight to c7. The Black king is then checked by White's queen. The king must move, and at the next turn, White is ready to capture the queen with the knight.

Discovered check!

Discovered checks have played a major role in many famous games. Let's look at one that created a sensation on and off the screen.

FROM RUSSIA WITH LOVE
BORIS SPASSKY VS. DAVID BRONSTEIN
PLAYED IN MOSCOW IN 1960

This brilliant game made such an impression that it was adapted for use in one of the early James Bond movies. It was used in a dramatic chess scene in *From Russia with Love*, though the film didn't actually credit the players, who were, of course, Russians. But not just any Russians! Ironically, the winner of this game was none other than Boris Spassky, who would go on to lose a celebrated world championship match against Bobby Fischer! His defeated opponent, David Bronstein, was the challenger in the 1951 World Championship, which he lost under circumstances that remain a mystery.

Boris Spassky

Spassky's attack is well underway. One of his knights has infiltrated at f7. The task now was to find a way to finish off his opponent's king. He starts by setting up a nasty discovered check.

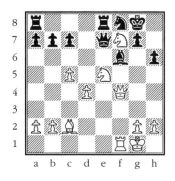

21.Bc2-b3

Bronstein could have escaped the discovered check by moving his king to h7, but that wouldn't help much. White would simply advance the queen to f5, giving check. Then, if Black blocks with the pawn, the bishop at f6 could be captured by the queen, supported by the rook at f1. If the knight blocks the check instead, it would be captured by the queen, guarded by the centralized knight at e5. So Bronstein decided to eliminate that knight.

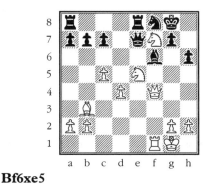

21...   **Bf6xe5**

22.Nf7xe5+

The knight avenges his mate's capture by taking the knight at e5 and opening up a discovered check at the same time. So this is another form of a capture-check.

22...   Kg8-h7

23.Qf4-e4+

The domination of two diagonals, combined with the power of the centralized knight and the rook on the open file was just too much.

Bronstein resigned. Black has an extra rook against a bishop and a pawn, but Black has no good answer to the check. If the knight moves to g6 to block, the queen captures with check, protected by the knight at e5. If the pawn blocks on the same square, the rook swoops down to f7, also guarded by the knight, and forks the king and queen. If Black retreats the king to h8, the rook captures the knight with check, and then the White knight goes to g6 and forks the king and queen.

The Windmill

In real life, windmills are useful things, peacefully delivering energy for people to use. In chess, however, the windmill is a weapon of mass destruction. Unleashing a windmill tactic against an opponent is usually a guarantee of victory.

The windmill is a series of discovered checks, with the piece uncovering the check returning to give check again after doing some destructive deed, usually capturing an enemy piece. It takes place when the opponent has no choice but to respond to the direct check by going back to its previous square, thus allowing another discovered check.

Watch how the Mexican champion Carlos Torre obliterates the defenses of the second world champion by offering up his queen in order to reach a windmill position.

CARLOS TORRE VS. EMMANUEL LASKER
PLAYED IN MOSCOW, RUSSIA IN 1925

25.Bg5-f6!!   Qb5xh5

Torre moved his bishop into position to set up the windmill at g7. Lasker, with queen under attack and undefended at b5, accepts the offering by capturing White's queen.

26.Rg3xg7+   Kg8-h8

In response to the capture of the pawn at g7 with check, the Black king has no alternative but to move to the corner square h8. On that square he is lined up with the bishop at f6, so when the rook moves, the king will be in check.

27.Rg7xf7+   Kh8-g8

Torre has captured a pawn with a discovered check. The king must return to g8. Torre will now repeat the procedure.

28.Rf7-g7+   Kg8-h8

Again, Lasker has no choice, but now Torre has a new discovered check, capturing the bishop at b7 and forcing the king to return to g8.

29.Rg7xb7+   Kh8-g8

Torre now returns the rook to g7 to set up the next discovered check.

30.Rb7-g7+   Kg8-h8

Torre could have grabbed another pawn by capturing at a7, but that pawn is of no real significance. Instead, the rook moves into a position where it attacks Black's queen.

31.Rg7-g5+   Kh8-h7

Finally, the king can get off the back rank; in fact, he doesn't have any choice. The king will take an active role in the hope of recovering some more material. Right now, Black has only a bishop and two pawns, once the rook takes the queen.

32.Rg5xh5   Kh7-g6

The king bravely forks the bishop at f6 and the rook at h5. Even if he only gets the bishop, the deficit can at least be reduced to just two pawns.

33.Rh5-h3   Kg6xf6

Unfortunately for Lasker, capturing the bishop with the king leaves the pawn at h6 undefended, and it can be captured with check.

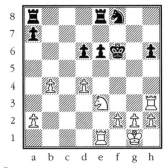

34.Rh3xh6+   Kf6-g5
35.Rh6-h3

The carnage is complete. Torre exploited his three-pawn advantage and won without difficulty.

The windmill is complete

Deflection and Decoy

Deflection and decoy are both used to reposition an enemy piece. Sometimes one of your opponent's pieces is in the way of your attack, and you need to get it out of the way. To do that, you use a deflection tactic. At other times, you want to lure an enemy piece into a specific position so that you can do something nasty to it.

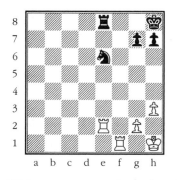

White wants to get the rook to f8

In this position, White would like to achieve a back-rank checkmate against Black's king. Unfortunately, the critical square, f8, is guarded by both a knight and a rook. White captures the knight.

Black cannot recapture

If Black captures the rook, White's remaining rook will deliver checkmate at f8. If Black does not capture, White's extra rook will surely lead to a win, and most players would resign.

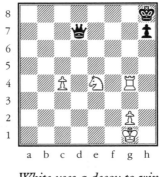

White uses a decoy to win

White's rook, knight and pawn balance Black's extra queen, but White quickly obtains a decisive advantage by decoying Black's king to g8, where it is subject to a fork by the knight moving to f6. The rook goes to g8 and gives check. Black must capture.

White uses a decoy to win.

Once the king is at g8, the knight wins the queen with a fork.

The fork finishes off the queen.

Once Black's queen is gone, White will eventually win after promoting one of the pawns to a new queen.

Deflections and decoys have artistic value, so it's not surprising that they turn up in many of the most highly praised games. Let's take a look at one of the more spectacular examples.

THE "PEARL OF ZANDVOORT"
MAX EUWE VS. ALEXANDER ALEKHINE
PLAYED IN ZANDVOORT, HOLLAND

This game was the 12th in the 1935 match for the world championship. Alekhine, defending his title, had a comfortable lead early on, but Euwe had closed the gap and needed a victory to pull even.

This is a complicated position. Notice that the knight at c6 is pinned to the rook at c1 by Black's queen. Black threatens to bring the rook up to b6, forking the White queen and the knight. If White loses that knight, the one-pawn advantage remaining might not be enough to secure victory. The real value of White's extra knight at the moment is that the knight at f1 guards the king, so that even if Black is able to capture the rook with the queen, at least it won't be with check.

34.Nc6xe7!   Qc7xe7

Euwe simply ignores the threat against the rook and captures the bishop defending the pawn at f6. The rook cannot be captured, because if the pawn at f6 is not defended, the White queen will capture it with checkmate! The queen must capture the knight, opening up the path to the back rank for the rook.

35.Rc1-c8+   Rb8xc8

Otherwise, White's rook would have captured Black's rook.

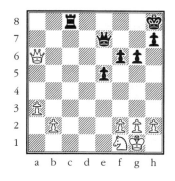

36.Qa6xc8+

Alekhine gave up, a full knight down and missing a pawn, as well.

Obey the Labor Laws!

An overworked defender is no defender at all! When the defensive burden is great, you can use decoys and deflections to force the piece to abandon its post.

One of the greatest exploitations of overworked pieces is seen in the following example.

THE POWER OF DISTANT FORCES
ROTLEVI VS. AKIBA RUBINSTEIN
PLAYED IN LODZ, POLAND

Black's attack is certainly worthy of respect. Material is even, and the queen is under attack at h4. After it moves to h3 or h5 to protect the knight, the bishop at b7 would fall. Obviously, Rubinstein must capture at e4 with check, and only after the recapture, presumably with the knight, the queen will retreat with about even chances, maybe a touch better for White. That's what Rotlevi must have been thinking. Boy, did he have a surprise coming: one of the most brilliant finishes of all time!

White's queen is overworked!

Take a closer look. The bishop at e4 is defended by both the knight and the queen. The knight at c3 can be removed by Black's rook at c8. The queen can't be captured, but it must remain in place to defend h2 against checkmate by the enemy queen. The rook at d8 can quickly join the attack at d2. That square is guarded by White's queen, but she is already burdened with responsibilities at h2 and e4.

22...   Rc8xc3!!

Black sacrifices the queen, leaves the knight at g4 hanging, and of course the bishop at c3 can be captured. What's going on? The obvious move for White is to capture the queen, and that's what Rotlevi does. If he had captured the rook at c3, Black would have used the bishop at b7 to capture the bishop at e4 with check. If the White queen captures the bishop, then Black's queen captures the pawn at h2, giving check. Rotlevi should have captured the bishop at b7 with the bishop at e4. In that case, Rubinstein would have captured the pawn at g3 with his rook. White's pawn at h2 is pinned by the Black queen, so it could not recapture. Rubinstein would surely have won the game, eventually.

23.g3xh4   Rd8-d2!!

Rubinstein has given up a queen, but his generosity does not stop there. Now another rook goes, while other pieces remain under enemy fire at g4, d2, c3 and b7.

24.Qe2xd2   Bb7xe4+

Rubinstein captures the unguarded bishop with check. The king cannot move to g1 because of the bishop at b6. White has no choice but to block.

25.Qd2-g2   Rc3-h3!

If Rubinstein had just settled for capturing the queen, White would only be at a small disadvantage. Instead, one more slice of inspiration brings about checkmate in four moves.

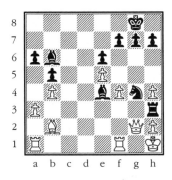

Rotlevi resigned.

All White can do is throw pieces away at d4, f2 or f3 to delay the execution.

There is No "Pass" in Chess

In some games, you have the option of skipping a turn, but in chess, if it is your move, you must make a legal move. This has tremendous importance in the endgame, as you will see later in the book. There are many positions where a player would not be in trouble if skipping a turn were permitted. In such positions, any move at all will give the opponent an opportunity to win.

This is known as *zugzwang*, a German word that has no English equivalent. It is one of those terms you need to know. The pronunciation of zugzwang is approximately TSUUG-TSVAHNG. But here's a tip. In chess conversation, you can just say *zuged*, as in "I zuged him."

Here is a simple example:

Black to move … and lose!

Black would have no problems at all if the king didn't have to move. All legal king moves leave the pawn at d6 to be captured by White's king. If Black could just sit and do nothing, everything would be fine. However, Black is in zugzwang and will lose the pawn, and eventually the game, all because the rules don't allow a "pass."

In the middlegame, it is also possible to find yourself in a position where any move you make will hurt your position, but if you could skip your turn there would be no problem.

THE "IMMORTAL ZUGZWANG" GAME
FRIEDRICH SAEMISCH VS. ARON NIMZOWITSCH
PLAYED IN COPENHAGEN, DENMARK, IN 1923

The most famous example of zugzwang in the middlegame is from a contest between two of the leading players of the Roaring Twenties.

Black to move

Let's take a look at White's position:

The knight has no safe move, because Black's pawn at b4 controls both a3 and c3.

The rook at e1 must stay in place to guard e2.

The rook at g1 cannot move to f1 because of Black's bishop at d3.

The bishop at d2 cannot retreat to c1 because then the knight at b1 would be captured.

The bishop at g2 cannot retreat to f1 because Black has three pieces attacking that square, and White has only two defenders.

The king must remain in the corner because if it moves up a square, the bishop at g2 will be pinned, and that would allow a Black rook to move to f3.

The queen cannot move to any safe square.

The pawn at d4 cannot advance.

White could advance the queenside pawns or the pawn at h3, but Black could simply make meaningless moves until those possibilities are exhausted.

Later on, we'll see what would happen if White advances the pawn from g3 to g4, attacking Black's rook. Right now, it's Black's move.

25...   h7-h6!!

Nimzowitsch has just advanced the pawn from h7-h6. Although this move doesn't have any particular function, Saemisch resigned! It is an example of inevitable zugzwang. If he just could sit and do nothing, Black has no immediate win. It might have been appropriate to play a few more moves, as the spectators may not have noticed that zugzwang is coming.

26.g3-g4   Rf5-f3

The advance of White's pawn to g4 opened the diagonal leading to h2. Sooner or later he would have no option but to advance the pawn from g3 to g4, allowing Nimzowitsch to carry out his plan. The queen has nowhere to run.

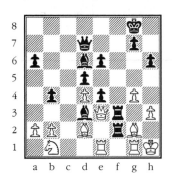

White would have had to capture the rook at f3, but that deflection takes away the blocker on the 2nd rank, and the rook can reach h2.

27.Bg2xf3   Rf2-h2#

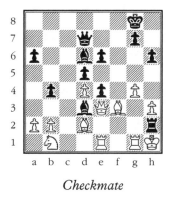

Checkmate

Four Keys to Tactical Thinking

Your opponent has just moved, and now it's your turn. Before you consider long-term strategy, it is very important to examine the position carefully for tactical opportunities, both for yourself and your opponent. The four keys to tactical thinking will go a long way to helping you discover the tactical resources in the position. Remember, chess is an interesting game precisely because making decisions is not simple. Still, you'll find the four keys will help you avoid mistakes and find ways to win that might otherwise escape your attention.

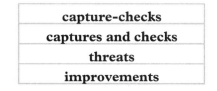

capture-checks
captures and checks
threats
improvements

We'll get into details on what each of these terms means, but first, there's something very important you must also remember. You must examine each of the possible candidate moves that meet the above criteria, even if some look absolutely ridiculous. Many of the greatest combinations in the history of the game started out with moves that most people would reject instantly. A move that sacrifices the queen, for example, is usually rejected because the enemy will capture a highly valued queen.

In order to develop your skill at finding tricky tactics, it is extremely important never to dismiss a candidate move simply on the basis of your opponent's immediate reply. Of course, when you're starting out in the game, you're not going to be able to see many moves in advance, but you'll quickly find that you can look at least two or three turns ahead.

To choose your move, you should first select a list of candidate moves. These are moves that you will pay special attention to. There is no point in looking at all of the legal moves, as there are often dozens. It takes too long to examine the ramifications of each move in detail, and it is a waste of time to consider moves that do not have any clear purpose. Most of the time, the correct move in any position will be one that meets one of the four criteria I've listed above. Now, let's look at the details.

Capture-Checks

Start by looking for all moves that are both a capture and a check. If a move is a check, it limits your opponent's options, because a check must be dealt with immediately. When there is also a capture involved, the move will also reap material rewards.

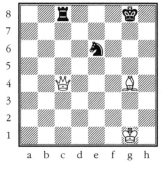

Capture checks available!

In this position, there are three capture-checks. Either the queen or the bishop can capture the knight at e6, giving check to the king and also attacking the rook. The queen can also capture the rook immediately with check. Any one of these moves would lead to the capture of both of Black's pieces.

Just because a capture-check is available doesn't mean that will be the best move. In the following position, it is clearly a very stupid move.

Don't capture!

White can capture the bishop with check, but would lose the queen! So obviously, that's a bad idea.

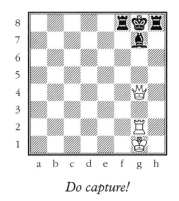

Do capture!

If the rook at a2 were at b2, the bishop could be captured, and Black would be in checkmate. In this case, your capture-check wins the game. Looking back at the previous position, you might conclude that moving your rook to g2 would be a good move. We'd then have this position, but with Black to move If Black didn't spot the threat, you could win the game.

Do capture!

This time I've added another attacker, the bishop at b2, and another defender, the knight at e8. At first it looks as though capturing the bishop with the queen would be a bad idea, because the knight could then capture the queen. But you must look deeper! Imagine the position after the knight captures:

Capture-check wins!

It is now White's turn, and the rook can capture the knight, giving checkmate because the rook is protected by the bishop at b2.

The following famous finish shows the value of a capture-check in its full glory.

THE "EVERGREEN" GAME

ADOLPH ANDERSSEN VS. JEAN DUFRESNE
PLAYED IN BERLIN, GERMANY, IN 1852

Anderssen has already sacrificed a knight for a pawn, but the pin on the knight at e7 seems to guarantee that he will regain it. Dufresne, taking notice of the pin on the pawn at g2, applied by the rook at g8, captures a second knight.

19.Qh5xf3?

Had Dufresne appreciated the danger, he might have tried a little sacrifice of his own, giving up his rook for the pawn at g2, hoping to unleash the power of the bishop at b7. Instead, he walked into a knockdown punch. Anderssen sacrifices the rook at e1 for the knight at e7. This is a powerful capture-check. It had to be a check, or Anderssen would have found himself checkmated at g2 by the enemy queen.

20.Re1xe7+!   Nc6xe7

Dufresne must have been happy here. He has a rook, queen and bishop aimed at g2, and his king seems perfectly safe. Anderssen appreciated the value of a capture-check, and did not fail to overlook the possibility of capturing the pawn at d7 with the queen. True, his opponent could simply capture the queen with the king. Then, however, the king would be lined up with the White rook at d1.

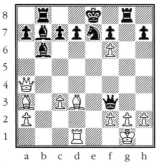

21.Qa4xd7+!!   Ke8xd7

Anderssen has only three attacking pieces left: the rook and a pair of bishops. The Black king seems to have plenty of possible defenders. Yet with precise play, Anderssen quickly finishes him off.

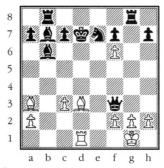

22.Bd3-f5+   Kd7-e8

If the king had gone to c6, the only other legal option, the bishop would move from f5 to d7, where, protected by the rook, it would deliver checkmate.

23.Bf5-d7+   Ke8-f8

If the king had moved to d8, Anderssen would have captured the knight with either bishop or pawn, giving checkmate in each case.

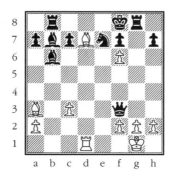

24.Ba3xe7#
The game ends with a capture-checkmate!

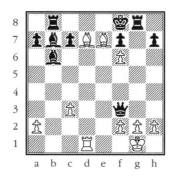

In the final position, Black has a queen and rook for two pawns, and threatens several checkmates. But Anderssen got there first, all because he used a series of capture-checks!

Captures and Checks

Checks and captures are also useful when applied independently. There is an old saying that suggests that you should always impose check because it might be checkmate, but that's not good advice. What you should do is examine all checks. Obviously, if the check happens to lead to checkmate, that's wonderful! But even if it doesn't, it still might be a good move because your opponent will have to respond to the check before doing anything else. Don't forget to include discovered checks, where one of your pieces checks the enemy king when another of your pieces gets out of the way!

Capturing enemy pieces is obviously useful, though you must avoid capturing just because you can. Capturing a piece might, in fact, fall in with your opponent's plan. Nevertheless, you must be aware of all possible captors, and take into consistent the effect they may have on the game. Remember to include discovered attacks in this category.

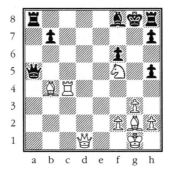

Find all the captures and checks

White has a lot of checks and captures available—ten—but only two lead to a checkmate in two moves. If you analyzed each of the possibilities, you'd surely wind up finding one of the two winners.

Queen to d5 gives check
Queen to g4 gives check
Rook to g4 gives check
Bishop to d5 gives check
Knight to e7 gives check
Knight to h6 gives check
Bishop at b4 can capture queen
Bishop at b4 can capture bishop
Bishop at g2 can capture pawn
Queen can capture pawn

If you examined carefully both the checks at d5, with queen or bishop, you probably found the winning plan. The only way Black can deal with the check at d5 is to capture the checking piece with the queen. In that case, whichever piece did not give the check would capture the Black queen at d5 with checkmate.

Since both captures and checks tend to limit the opponent's options, it is easier to calculate the consequences. A series of captures and checks can be extremely effective, as we see in a famous game.

PUMMELING YOUR OPPONENT WITH CAPTURES AND CHECKS

FRANK MARSHALL VS. COLONEL MOREAU
PLAYED IN MONTE CARLO, MONACO, IN 1903

Both kings are under attack. Black threatens checkmate in one move by capturing at g2 with the queen, protected by the pawn at f3. Black's king has some security provided by three pawns, but White is attacking the pawn at d6 with three different pieces. White also threatens the rook at h8, but with his own king under assault, can't spare the time to capture it.

21.Rd1xd6+   c7xd6

Marshall starts by sacrificing a rook at d6, where it captures a pawn with check. After Black recaptures, it looks as though the king is relatively safe behind the barrier of pawns. The pawn that just arrived at d6, however, is swiftly swept from the board, because White has both knight and queen attacking it.

22.Qe5xd6+   Kd7-c8

After White captures the pawn with the queen, giving check, Black's king retreats. Notice that if it were Black's turn here, the pawn at g2 would be captured by the queen, and White would be in checkmate. White must continue to give check in order to avoid the checkmate.

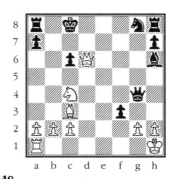

23. Qd6xc6+   Kc8-d8

24. Ra1-d1+   Kd8-e7

The king has no choice, because White's queen controls all the other flight squares. Another pawn falls with check, and White could now capture either of the rooks. The bishop at c3 attacks the rook at h8, and the queen at c6 can capture the rook at a8 with check. However, when you're trying to checkmate your opponent, it is usually helpful to have all of your pieces participate in the attack. So White must also consider giving check with the bishop at a5, or with the rook, by moving it to d1. Since the bishop is already in the game, White brings the rook into the attack.

25.Qc6-d6+ Ke7-e8

Black's king has no defenders in the neighborhood, though the queen and the knight guard a few important squares at d7, e6, e7 and f6. Marshall keeps pounding away.

26.Rd1-e1+ Ke8-f7

The king is forced to a square where it can be checked by the knight.

27.Nc4-e5+ Kf7-e8

28.Ne5-g6+   Bh6 e3

Marshall could now simply capture Black's queen with discovered check, but there is a better move. With the rook giving check along the e-file, Black has no choice but to place a piece in the way. If the king moves to f7, the game ends when the knight captures the rook in the corner, checkmating him. It is very rare that you win a game of chess by moving your knight to a corner square!

29.Re1xe3+   Qg4-e6

Again there is no choice. Blocking with the knight allows capture with checkmate. The Black queen no longer threatens checkmate, and the rest is easy.

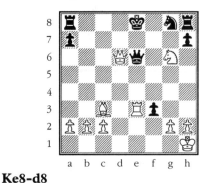

30.Qd6xe6+   Ke8-d8

One queen captures another, and the king is forced to move. If Black had blocked with the knight, the queen would have captured the knight with checkmate.

31.Bc3-a5#

The bishop finally manages to toss in a check, and it is checkmate.

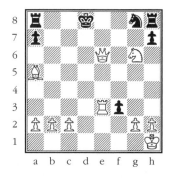

 WORST RESULTS

Colonel Moreau holds a special place in the history of chess, though not a coveted one. He managed to lose all 26 of his games in this event.

Threats

Even if you can't capture or give check right away, you can create a threat of doing so on your next turn. When you create a threat, you also limit your opponent's options, so you have less to calculate. A single threat is not as useful as a fork, but sometimes it can be just as effective.

White's pieces are forked

It looks like White is in trouble. Black has forked his bishop and rook. However, the rook can move to b6, attacking Black's undefended bishop.

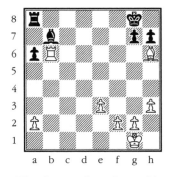

The threat solves the problem

When Black captures the bishop at h6, White will grab the bishop at b7. If Black saves his bishop, the White bishop can escape to a safe square. In either case, White's extra pawns should win in the end.

Improve a Piece's Position

If you don't have a winning check, capture or threat, try to improve the position of an attacked piece, or one that is doing nothing of importance. Look for inactive pieces and see if you can move them to more useful positions.

The rook needs a job!

In this very simple position, White's rook at c1 isn't doing anything. The rook at f2 at least is preventing the king from going to the queenside to help deal with the advanced pawn at a6. That pawn is under attack. So, the rook at c1 can be put to use guarding the pawn at a6, by moving to a1 or c6. Going to c6 would be the better choice, because it also attacks Black's pawn at g6.

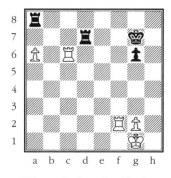

The rook does double duty.

By the way, the rook is not overworked, despite having two tasks. Attacking doesn't count as work. It is too much fun!

You may have noticed that I haven't said anything about retreating. Many beginners think that if your piece is attacked, the first thing you should do is figure out how to avoid losing it. In fact, defending an attacked piece is not always a high priority. That's why I suggest looking at all your offensive options before worrying about saving one of your pieces. However, you must never forget about your opponent's threat!

Escape is the only option

In this position, there are no checks, the capture at a8 is out of the question because the rook there is protected by its colleague at f8, and there are no serious threats against enemy forces. So obviously, you would move your queen to a safe square. This is the best plan, but even so, running away should be considered only when there isn't a better option.

If you take care to examine all possible captures, checks and threats before settling for improving the position of one of your pieces, you'll have much better success at the board. You'll find, however, that it takes extraordinary mental discipline to do that, and few players are capable of doing it, especially when there is a time limit on the moves.

Planning and Plotting

If tactics are the down-to-earth business of chess, strategy is its fine art. Creativity is needed. It is well known the computers do not do well at long-term planning in chess. They can crunch numbers, but they cannot dream. And indeed, dreaming is what is necessary to organize your thoughts and take into consideration all of the important factors on the chessboard.

I believe in Magic....There is Magic in the creative faculty such as great poets and philosophers conspicuously possess, and equally in the creative Chessmaster.
—*Emanuel Lasker, 2ⁿᵈ World Champion*

When you are trying to develop a long-range plan, it's useful to fantasize about the position. This is best done when it is your opponent's turn, especially if you are playing with a clock. Try imagining the tactical operations that could be carried out if it weren't for the presence of a certain piece. Forget about the laws of chess for a moment, and think about where you would like to put your pieces if you could simply pick them up and move them to any square on the board. Imagine your opponent could not move, or was simply moving one piece back and forth.

Once you check out the possibilities and figure out what you might want to do, all you have to do is find some way to make your dream a reality by repositioning your forces. Tactical devices, including sacrifices, can help get you where you want to go.

Don't give up on a plan just because your opponent seems to have some move that can thwart it. Keep looking, because maybe you can find a way to eliminate that defensive resource. Once you do develop a strategy, it's usually a good idea to stick to it unless your opponent is creating serious threats. So, choosing a strategy is one of your most important tasks.

If you haven't played much chess, most of your games will be decided by tactics, not strategy. But as you progress and face stronger opposition, you'll find that these tactical mistakes are less frequent. Then the strategy becomes the center of the contest.

Our example involves a position where White's back rank inspires dreams of a back rank checkmate.

EXPLOITING THE BACK RANK

OSIP BERNSTEIN VS. JOSE CAPABLANCA
PLAYED IN MOSCOW, RUSSIA, IN 1914

At first glance, this seems to be a quite simple position where White has the advantage of one extra pawn, but it isn't in a position to cause any harm. However, the placement of the rook at c3 is not good. It should be back on c1, defending White's back rank. The weakness of the back rank is the key flaw in many games.

Black has a crushing move!

The back rank is not completely defenseless. The White queen at e2 guards three important squares on her home rank, and can retreat to f1 to block a check.

In fact, Black has to be careful not to overplay the position. His own back rank is also weak, defended only by the rook at d8. For example, if Black were to give check with the queen at b1, White would bring the queen back to f1 to block. Then, if Black falls for the trap, he'll move the rook from d8 to d1. That looks fatal, because White's queen is attacked and pinned to the king, and if she captures the rook, Black's queen will capture her with checkmate.

However, if the game followed this path, after the Black rook moves to d1, White's rook would move to c8, giving check. Black would have no choice but to retreat his own rook, which would then be captured by White's rook, with checkmate.

29...   **Qb6-b2!!**

Bernstein probably didn't anticipate this reply. Capablanca has moved the queen into a position where she can be captured by the enemy queen. Then, however, Black's rook would come down to d1 with checkmate. Meanwhile, both the queen at c2 and rook at c3 are attacked.

Bernstein resigned, because if he moved the queen to protect the rook, for example at d1, Capablanca would grab the rook anyway. When the queen recaptures, Black's rook would invade the home rank at d1. White would have to block with the queen at e1, and the queen would then be captured with checkmate.

Checkmate is the obvious goal of chess strategy, but there are many other concrete objectives that require strategic planning. Let's take a look at a few of the most important considerations.

Balance of Power

It is a lot easier to checkmate the enemy king when you have a bigger army. So, if you can capture enemy pieces without losing any of your own, you'll find it a lot easier to win. The balance of power in chess is calculated according to the values of the pieces. Remember, winning the fight for the balance of power is a strategic goal, but you have to make sure that the pieces are in useful positions.

Compensation

"A rook on the seventh rank is sufficient compensation for a pawn."
—Reuben Fine

When the balance of power favors one side, the other side might have compensation that makes up for the missing pawns or pieces. This compensation can take many forms. The player with the smaller army might have a strong attack, or might have pieces in particularly useful positions. Perhaps the side with the greater power has weaknesses in the king position, or in the pawn formation. If you sacrifice a piece but gain some significant benefits in return, it's like playing a gambit in the opening. Just make sure you get something for your investment!

Defense

A good defense is an important part of successful chess strategy. You may come up with a very inventive and powerful attacking scheme, but if your own king and forces are not sufficiently defended, the enemy may get in first.

Hence that general is skilful in attack whose opponent does not know what to defend; and he is skilful in defense whose opponent does not know what to attack.
— *Sun Tzu*

KEEP AN EYE ON THE WHOLE BOARD
SAMMY RESHEVSKY VS. VLADIMIR SAVON
PLAYED IN PETROPOLIS, BRAZIL IN 1973

Remember the bishop at b1!

Black's king is under attack, and seems to have only the trio of pawns as defenders. But off in the distance, at b1, sits the long-range bishop! In time trouble, Reshevsky failed to notice him, and the result is a catastrophe.

39.Qe8xf7+   Kh7-h6

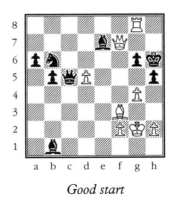

Good start

Reshevsky started with a capture-check, the first candidate move. When you are short of time, a capture-check is always tempting. This time, it was correct. The king is driven to the edge of the board, where it can be checkmated.

40.Qf7xg6+??

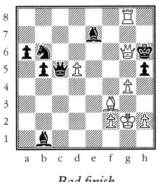

Bad finish

Not this way! True, the move is a capture-check, but it ignores the defender at b1. Savon captured the queen at g6, and Reshevsky gave up.

Suppose, however, Reshevsky had also considered the check by the g-pawn.

Little pawn, big attack!

40. g4-g5+   Kh6xg5

Black would have to capture the pawn, as there is no retreat because of the queen at f7. White could now offer the h-pawn as a sacrifice.

41. h2-h4+   Kg5xh4

If the king retreats to h6, White moves the rook to h8 and it is checkmate.

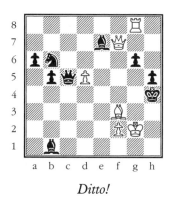

Ditto!

42. Qf7-f4#

Reshevsky would then have delivered checkmate at f4, and would have won the game! Such errors are not uncommon when players are under extreme time pressure.

King Safety

Above all, you must protect your king. It would probably be fitting if an arbiter, at the start of the game, said to the players, "Remember to protect your king at all times," just as boxers are instructed to protect themselves at all times. It doesn't matter how many advantages your position holds if your king is checkmated.

I would give all my fame for a pot of ale and safety.
—William Shakespeare, Henry V

One of the reasons it is so important to castle is that castling protects the pawn at f7, assuming Black is castling kingside. That square is the most vulnerable area in each player's camp at the start of the game. After castling, the main weakness is usually the pawn on the h-file. However, even if you have castled, there is still plenty of danger at the traditional target on f7.

Consider the next example, where a future world champion defeats a former world champion.

WEAKNESS AT F7
MIKHAIL TAL VS. VASSILY SMYSLOV
PLAYED IN BLED, YUGOSLAVIA, IN 1959

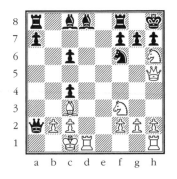

Tal's attack is going nicely. He can take the pawn at f7 with the knight, but that hardly makes sense with the queen under attack, even if the pawn does fall with check. After the king moves to g8, he has too many problems to solve. So, "The Magician" uncorks a powerful queen sacrifice.

19.Qh5xf7!!

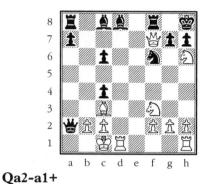

19...   **Qa2-a1+**

Smyslov had to decline the offer. If he captured the queen with the rook, White would have taken the rook at d1 and captured Black's bishop at d8 with check. Then, if Black's knight retreated to g8 to block the check, Tal would have had an amusing choice: capturing the knight with the rook, delivering checkmate, or taking the rook at f7 (where it captured the White queen), with a smothered mate!

    20.Kc1-d2   **Rf8xf7**

Now White cannot capture the bishop at d8 with check because the king at d2 stands in the way.

    21.Nh6xf7+   **Kh8-g8**

The Black king is no longer in any danger, but his queen at a1 falls to White's rook.

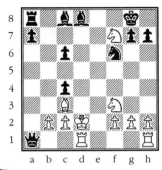

22.Rd1xa1   Kg8xf7

After a series of forced exchanges, Tal has a winning endgame. Smyslov didn't resist for long after another pawn fell, and Tal emerged with a victory.

Breathing Room

A cramped position contains the seeds of defeat.
—Siegbert Tarrasch

Another important element of king safety is ensuring that your king has some room to breathe, or someplace to run, if necessary. For example, when your king is on the back rank in a castled position, it is often useful to advance the rook's pawn so that the possibility of a back-rank checkmate is reduced.

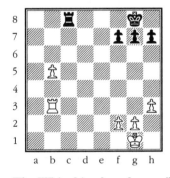

The White king breathes easily

White doesn't have to worry about Black's rook giving check on the back rank because an escape square is available at h2.

The Walls (pawn structure)

Take care of the Pawns and the Queens take care of themselves.
—*Samuel Loyd*

Attacks on your major pieces require open lines, which means that the defending pawns have been cleared out of the way. If you are defending, you want to keep the pawn barrier intact so that it can continue to protect your territory. When you create weaknesses in your pawn structure, these attract the attention of your opponent, who will figure out a way to exploit them.

Backward Pawns

A backward pawn is one that has no neighboring pawn on a rank behind it to offer support. Pawns like to be supported by other pawns, and may be difficult to maintain if they have to rely on pieces instead. A backward pawn can have no such support. It is doomed to live its life as a weakling, ever a target for enemy forces. Some backward pawns are more of a liability than others, but they are always weak.

The weakling and the coward are out of place in a strong and free community.
—*Theodore Roosevelt*

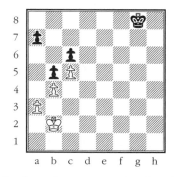

Backward pawns at a3, a7 and c6

In the diagram above, both sides have backward pawns. White has a backward pawn at a3, guarded by the king. Black has a backward pawn at c6 and another one at a7. The backward pawns at c6 and a7 aren't much of a problem as long as Black keeps the White king from invading. However, when more pieces are on the board, a backward pawn can be attacked easily.

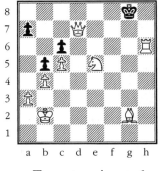

Target practice at c6

The weak backward pawn can be attacked from many directions by many different pieces. That's why it is considered a liability.

Doubled Pawns

Pawns are doubled when they sit on the same file. They have been traditionally considered a weakness, though they aren't considered a major liability unless they are isolated.

Only the pawn at c6 is weak

Doubled pawns are especially weak when they are isolated. Without the support of neighboring pawns, they are difficult to defend. When the doubled pawns are part of what should be a healthy pawn barrier protecting the king, the consequences can be fatal.

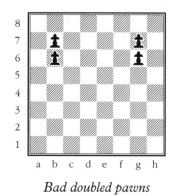

Bad doubled pawns

Doubled pawns are weak in many cases, but strong in some, so you should evaluate each case on its own merits. It is safest to accept doubling of your pawns when you can comfortably capture toward the center, as this does not bring with it the likelihood of a losing king-and-pawn endgame.

Triangles

A triangle of pawns can be strong or weak, depending on whether there is any piece available to patrol the squares of the color opposite to those the pawns sit on.

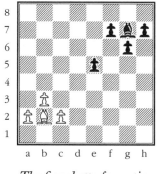

The fianchetto formation

A triangle formation is strong as long as there is a bishop at home. If the bishop is exchanged, very bad things can happen. The triangle is the base of operations for many opening strategies, including the King's Indian Defense and the Dragon Sicilian. In the latter, the bishop is needed both for defense and to attack the enemy queenside.

♔ ♕ **HELPFUL TIP**

The triangle formation with a bishop in the neighborhood, especially in the ideal position shown above, is known as a *fianchetto* (FEE-ANN-KET-TO), borrowed from Italian. That term only applies when the triangle is anchored on the second rank.

Holes

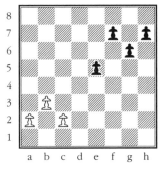

Lots of potholes on the road!

A hole is a square near enemy pawn formations which cannot be defended by an enemy pawn. Holes are significant at every stage of the game. When a hole is occupied by a piece, we call it an outpost, because it represents a safe haven deep inside enemy territory. A couple of holes can easily lead to checkmate.

Weak points or holes in the enemy position must be occupied by pieces, not pawns
—Siegbert Tarrasch

It is often tempting to place a pawn on a weak square in the enemy position, but such holes are better occupied by pieces. A pawn has control only over the two squares diagonally in front of it.

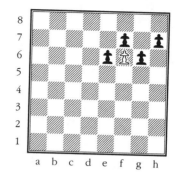

The pawn at f6 is useful of course, but the effect is limited by the short range. Black is deprived of two squares, and the pawn cannot reposition itself to inflict any serious damage.

A knight has a much greater effect because it attacks four points in the enemy position.

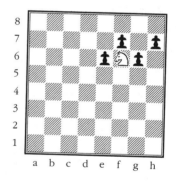

The knight would fork any two pieces on d7, e8, g8 and h7, possibly also enemy pieces to the rear at e5, h5, d5 and e4. It can move to any of those eight squares and reposition itself for another attack, should the immediate occupation at f6 not bring the desired result.

Bishops can be very powerful when operating from a hole in the enemy position. There are many checkmating patterns that involve a bishop on this square, as you will see in the inventory of mating positions in the Tactics chapter.

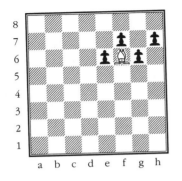

You can see that the bishop controls key squares at e7, g7, h8 and d8. The bishop does not have the ability to attack squares of both colors, so is somewhat more limited than the knight in this regard.

Because holes are, by definition, close to the enemy home rank, the queen is less effective than minor pieces in a hole. Often she can be chased away easily. In any case, the queen only adds an additional two squares to the coverage of the bishop: f7 and g6. Of course, if the f-file is open for use by a rook, the pressure on f7 can be intense.

A rook, powerful as it is, is almost useless when occupying a hole. It is surrounded by well-defended pawns. In general, a rook in a hole is not positioned better than a rook safely stationed farther back on the file.

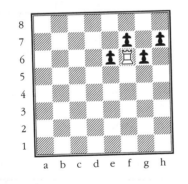

In general, therefore, try to occupy holes with minor pieces.

The Isolated d-pawn

I'm lonely!

Entire books have been devoted to discussion of the strengths and weaknesses of the isolated d-pawn. Many important opening strategies crucially revolve around this pawn.

An isolated Pawn spreads gloom all over the chessboard.
—Savielly Tartakower

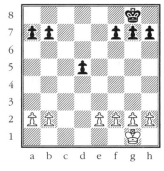

Typical isolated d-pawn position

If the game came down to a king-and-pawn endgame, Black would likely be lost. The pawn at d5 is weak, and can easily be blockaded by an enemy king at d4. In fact, the blockade is the best known strategy for operating against an isolated d-pawn. The best blockaders are pieces of limited mobility and value, so a knight is ideal in that role.

The pawn is blockaded

When there is a White piece at d4, the Black pawn cannot advance from d5, and White can aim other pieces at it. A blockade is a potent weapon against the isolated pawn, rendering it very weak. On the other hand, the isolated pawn is a source of dynamic strength, because it cramps the enemy position. In the position above, White cannot make use of the c4 or e4 squares.

The strength of an isolated pawn lies in its lust to expand.
—Aron Nimzowitsch

An isolated d-pawn on the fourth rank does indeed feel a powerful urge to get to the fifth rank. The pawn does not feel comfortable on the fourth rank, where it can be blocked by one enemy piece and then attacked from all sides. Advancing the pawn can be effective even when it merely seems to simplify the position. The advance of the isolated pawn is not just a way of getting rid of the nuisance. Since the holder of an isolated d-pawn often enjoys an advantage in space, the elimination of the pawn can increase that factor and result in a substantial advantage.

TIPS ON ISOLATED PAWNS

If you have an isolated pawn, you must consider whether the advance of the pawn, and offer of exchange, will improve your position. If you release the tension too soon, you will be left with mere equality. If you wait too long, you'll be stuck with a sick pawn in the endgame.

When playing against the isolated pawn, try to blockade it with a piece and control the neighboring files. Then you can try to win it. Do not rush the attack on the isolated pawn. As the game progresses it becomes weaker and more vulnerable.

Hanging Pawns

Hanging pawns are adjacent pawns with no means of support. They can be defended by pieces, but have no pawns to give them the protection they sometimes need. They are easy to attack by rooks lined up on the open lines in front of the pawns.

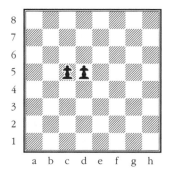

Because the hanging pawns cannot be protected by other pawns, they must be supported by pieces. If the defending pieces are eliminated, or sufficient force is brought to bear, the pawns can be captured.

Handling hanging pawns takes a great deal of care, and is a task best left to professionals. You should avoid hanging pawns because they tie down your pieces in defense. When your opponent has hanging pawns, look for ways to attack in other areas of the board.

Passed Pawns

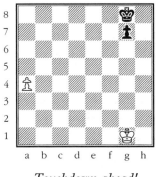

Touchdown ahead!

A pawn is **passed** when there is no pawn obstructing its path to the promotion square, either on the same file or an adjacent one. In the diagram, White's pawn is passed, and there is no way to stop it from promoting. It will reach the 8th rank in just four moves.

A passed pawn increases in strength as the number of pieces on the board diminishes
—Jose Capablanca, 3rd World Champion

Each time a piece is captured there is one less resource to be used in stopping a pawn from marching up the board. That's why you should try to exchange pieces when you have a passed pawn. Reduce the number of potential defenders and you will have a significant advantage.

Keep in mind that when you have only one pawn, your opponent can sacrifice a piece to remove it, and will often achieve a draw as a result. This defensive plan is the key to many endgames.

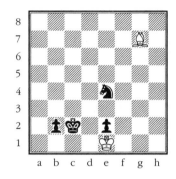

Black threatens to make a new queen

Things look bad for White, but there is an escape. White captures the pawn at b2. If the king captures the bishop, the White king grabs the e-pawn and the game is drawn because Black has insufficient checkmating material. If Black ignores the bishop at b2 and protects the pawn by moving the knight to g3, White moves the bishop to e5, attacking the knight. This will also result in a draw, assuming White doesn't do something very foolish.

The passed pawn is a criminal, who should be kept under lock and key; mild measures, such as police surveillance, are not sufficient
— *Aron Nimzowitsch*

Your opponent's passed pawn can be your worst nightmare. In the endgame, preventing a passed pawn from reaching the promotion square is one of your most crucial tasks. The best defense is to keep it rooted to its square, unable to advance. That is what Nimzowitsch means by being "under lock and key." The surveillance he refers to means, use pieces to control squares that lie between the pawn's current location and the promotion square.

Pawn Chains

Pawn chains are groups of pawns that are connected to pawns on adjacent files. They can be static, as in the case of stonewall formations, or dynamic, advancing to attack the enemy position. A pawn chain can look like this.

Pawns are born free, yet are everywhere in chains.
—Grandmaster Andrew Soltis

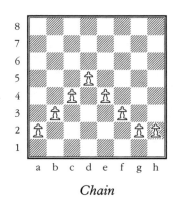

Chain

We rarely encounter such a long chain, but pawn chains are characteristic of certain openings. Chains consist of at least three pawns, and can have different shapes.

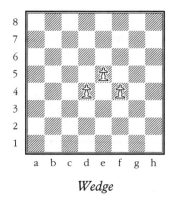

Wedge

A three-pawn chain facing forward is called a wedge or a triangle. But even if there were a bishop at e4, it wouldn't be called a fianchetto. For that, the triangle must be on the second rank.

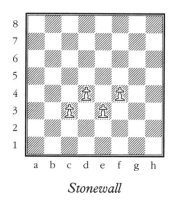

Stonewall

This is a stonewall. Although it presents a formidable barrier, there are lots of windows that pieces can move through. It is important to try to control those squares, because they are holes in the wall.

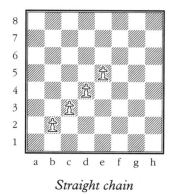

Straight chain

The straight chain is one of the strongest formations, because the only weak pawn is the one on the second rank. This pawn anchors the chain, but even if it is lost, the chain would still be intact, just smaller, with its base on the third rank.

Fun Along the Seventh Rank

One of the most effective attacking techniques is to invade the 7th rank (the opponent's second rank) with a rook or queen. Enemy forces along that rank are especially vulnerable to attack by such invaders. Here is an instructive example.

7ᵀᴴ RANK RULES AT HASTINGS

STEINITZ VS. VON BARDELEBEN
PLAYED IN HASTINGS, ENGLAND, IN 1895

22.Re1xe7+!   Ke8-f8

Capturing with the queen would lose, because the White rook at c1 would capture its counterpart on c8. Then after the rook on the corner recaptures, the white Queen would swoop in from g4 and capture again at c8. That capture would come with check, as well. On the other hand, if Black captures with the king, White gives check with the rook at e1.

Then the king must move, but to a square where it can protect the queen, because she is under attack from g4. If the king retreats to d8, White moves the knight to e6, giving check and forcing the Black king to go back to the e-file. Then the knight could move away to c5, with a discovered check from the rook at e1. No matter what Black does, White would capture the queen on the next turn.

Finally, the king can try to flee to d6, but then White moves the queen from g4 over to b4, creating all sorts of problems with a deadly check. So, Von Bardeleben decided to leave the rook where it is. He had a clever trick in mind.

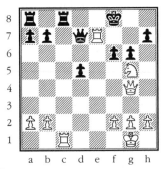

23.Re7-f7+!   Kf8-g8

Steinitz avoided the trap. If he had captured Black's queen, the rook at c8 would capture the rook at c1 with a back-rank checkmate. The king is in check, but Black still couldn't capture the rook with the queen, because then the rook at c8 would not have enough protection. So, he slid the king over to g8. The rook has only begun to have fun on the 7th rank, and the hits just keep on coming!

24.Rf7-g7+!   Kg8-h8

This monster cannot be killed! If Black captures with the king, Steinitz grabs the queen at d7 with check, and Black cannot hold out for long. On the other hand, if the queen captures the rook, there is the usual problem at c8. Finally, the king had to go to the corner rather than back to f8, because if the king moves back toward the center, White's knight at g5 will capture the pawn at h7 with check. If the king captures the rook at f7, Steinitz would again have the opportunity to capture the enemy queen with check.

25.Rg7xh7+   Kh8-g8

Von Bardeleben actually resigned after White's move, not wanting to provide Steinitz the pleasure of a beautiful finish, though it was a bit unsporting of him not to allow the public to see the logical conclusion to the masterpiece. Let's see what would have happened had he moved the king to g8 in an attempt to play on.

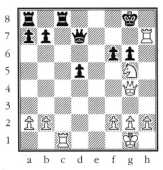

26.Rh7-g7+!   Kg8-h8

Once again, moving the king to f8 would be met by the capture of the h-pawn by the knight, with check. Capturing the rook with the queen would allow Steinitz to finish off the rook at c8. So Black must return to h8. But now the queen enters the attack via the opened h-file:

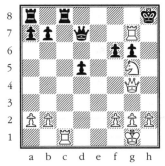

27.Qg4-h4+!   Kh8xg7

This capture is forced because it is the only legal move.

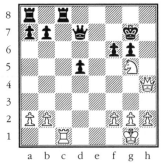

28.Qh4-h7+   Kg7-f8

Again, Black has no choice.

29.Qh7-h8+   Kf8-e7

The king cannot go to f7 because that square is covered by the knight at g5.

30.Qh8-g7+   Ke7-e8

If the king had gone to d6 instead, White would simply capture the pawn at f6 with the queen, giving check, and Black would have no choice but to block with the queen. Then, White's queen would capture Black's queen with checkmate.

31.Qg7-g8+   Ke8-e7

White's queen creeps closer, but Black can do nothing, because there is only one legal move available.

32.Qg8-f7+   Ke7-d8

If the king had gone to d6, he would have met the same fate as if he had gone there earlier.

33.Qf7-f8+   Qd7-e8

Finally, the king can sit still while his queen retreats to block the check. White could move the queen to d6, giving check, but then Black could still block with the queen, at d7. However, a check delivered by a knight cannot be blocked. Steinitz brings in the knight to help finish off the game.

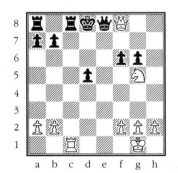

34.Ng5-f7+   Kd8-d7
35.Qf8-d6#

The king is finally checkmated. Steinitz had to carry out his attack using a check at every turn. Even in the final position, notice that Black's rook on c8 threatens to capture White's rook on c1 with checkmate. So, if Steinitz had made a move that wasn't a check, while the rook was still sitting unprotected at c1, it is Black who would have won the game.

Four Keys to Strategic Planning

You've already seen the four keys to good opening play and tactical play; now let's add four keys to strategic planning. These four tips will help you find moves that are appropriate to the position and can help lead to victory.

Find the weak spots
Avoid weaknesses
Eliminate defenders
Capablanca's rule

Find the Weak Spots!

Look for weak points in your opponent's position. Is the enemy king safe? Are there holes in the pawn structure? Are some of the pieces or pawns undefended? Search the enemy position for any vulnerabilities you can exploit.

Both sides have weaknesses

Black has a lot of problems in this position. The queenside and center pawns are weak, and the knight can be vulnerable if the knight at d4 gets out of the way of the bishop. The knight can move to c6, but Black has more firepower aimed at that square. Black's king has to keep an eye out for problems on the back rank, since he has no escape square.

White, on the other hand, has weak pawns at b2 and g4. This gives Black some chances to create counterplay. For example, assuming it is Black's turn, the knight can be moved to c6, White can exchange knights and then capture the pawn that lands on c6 with the rook. In this case, Black will be able to capture the weak pawn at g4, since the pawn from d7 got out of the when it captured White's knight at c6.

However, if it is White's move, a pawn advance from h2-h3 would eliminate the possibility of that trick. Even better, the knight can go to b5. If Black captures the knight, White recaptures with the pawn, which cannot be captured by the rook since the rook must stay at b8 to guard the bishop once the knight is gone from a7. If, after Nd4-b5, Black plays …Na7-c6, White can exploit the weak dark squares by shifting the bishop to f4.

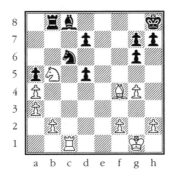

The weak dark squares are exploited

Black would then be in a bad position. The rook must stay on the back rank, or else the White rook will move to e1 with the deadly threat of a back-rank checkmate. So the rook would have to go to a8, and then White would fork the rook and weak pawn at d5 by moving the knight to c7.

Black is forked

You can spot such tricks by keeping in mind the weak spots that provide good targets for your pieces.

Avoid Weaknesses

Avoid weaknesses in your own position, as they will give you opponent opportunities. Take special care of your pawn structure, since it is hard to repair. Keep your king safe at all times.

Solid positions

Both sides have solid positions with no apparent weaknesses. It is not easy to come up with effective attacking strategies is positions like this. Any attempt at a direct attack will necessarily involve making some sort of weakness in the position.

This is one of chess's balancing acts. On the one hand, you want to keep your position solid. On the other hand, to attack, you will need to make some sort of concession. When both positions are solid, you'll need to allow a weakness. In the position above, White could move the knight from f3 to e5, followed by advancing the pawn from f2 to f4. This is known as a "stonewall" attack. White will have a weak pawn at e3, but that is the price to be paid for the strong control of e5 and a potential kingside attack. Fortunately, the little weakness is close to home, and the backward pawn at e3 can be defended easily.

So, create as few weaknesses as possible, and try to make sure they can be defended or, in the case of weak pawns, perhaps sacrificed for the good of the attack.

Eliminate Defenders

Try to eliminate defenders of the enemy king. Then, your attack can proceed without serious opposition. If the enemy king is guarded by a strong contingent of forces, you have to get them out of the way. You can use sacrifices to accomplish this task. Here is a simple example.

1.Rf1xf6!

Eliminate the defender of h7!

With the knight at f6 gone, Black can't defend the pawn at h7, targeted by the White queen with the support of the bishop. Black can't defend against the checkmate and capture the rook at the same time, White has won the knight for free, since the rook can retreat on the next turn.

Capablanca's Rule

Capablanca's rule is quite simple. You need to attack with more force than your opponent can muster to defend. For the most part, chess is not a game of superheroes. A single piece can only do so much. You need to bring a squadron to attack the enemy king. Unless you want to rely on luck, you need to make sure that your attacking force is greater than your opponent's defensive resources.

Here is a good attacking position, from a game between Garry Kasparov and 6-time U.S. Champion, Walter Browne.

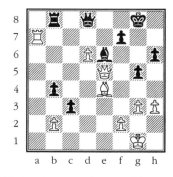

White's pieces are in attacking positions

Kasparov's queen and bishop are aiming toward the Black king, and the rook at a7 controls the seventh rank. The future world champion won brilliantly by playing 1.Bd4-h7+ Kg8xh7 and then Qe5xe6, exploiting a pin.

There is no way to prevent White from capturing the pawn at f7 on the next turn, and Black resigned this hopeless position.

On the other hand, the following attack, often seen in games by beginners, is not likely to succeed.

Bad attack

The Black king is surrounded by defenders, and the only attacker is a queen. Of course, Black can stumble into oblivion with 2...Ke8-e7?, allowing checkmate at e5. However, after the simple move 2...Nb8-c6!, the pawn at e5 is defended. Then, if White persists in the attack with 3.Bf1-c4, threatening the "Scholar's Mate." Black can simply chase the queen away by advancing the pawn to g6, or can defend f7 by moving the queen.

Don't launch a direct attack unless you can bring sufficient force to overwhelm the defense! Place your pieces in attacking positions, and when you have gathered sufficient force, your attack can really get going.

CHAPTER 8
The Endgame

To be capable of conducting an endgame to the distant goal with clarity,
firmness, and complete familiarity with all its tricks and traps is the sign
of the first-class master.
—*Grandmaster Jacques Mieses*

There is no strict definition of the endgame. It begins when the middlegame
ends, usually when all thoughts of directly checkmating the opposing king have
been replaced by a new goal: promoting a pawn to create a new queen who will be
able to deliver the checkmate. That shift in strategic goal can take place even when
there are quite a few pieces on the board. Many people feel comfortable using the
term "endgame" to describe any position where the queens are gone. (Of course, if
each side has just a queen and two or three other pieces or pawns, that's clearly an
endgame.)

Pawn endings are to chess what putting is to golf.
—*Cecil Purdy*

Because the endgame involves a different kind of strategy, let's take a look
at various aspects of the endgames, and then I'll give you the four keys to good
endgame play.

Play the opening like a book, the middle game like a magician, and the
endgame like a machine.
—*Grandmaster Rudolph Spielmann*

Checkmate is the Goal

Of course, checkmate remains the overall strategic goal, and you'll find there are plenty of ways of checkmating an enemy king when there are few pieces on the board. However, if the balance of power is about even, a checkmate isn't too likely. You'll need to upset the balance, either by capturing enemy pieces or getting a new queen. In the middlegame, you aren't likely to escort a pawn to the 8th rank, so capturing enemy pieces is a more reasonable goal. In the endgame, the roles are reversed.

In an endgame, both sides start out with reduced force, usually less than the value of a queen and a pair of rooks, not counting pawns. Therefore, both offensive and defensive force is limited, and unless you can capture some of the opposition, direct attacks are not likely to work. However, the possibility of getting a new queen is important. We'll look at that next, but first, let's see what factors might allow a checkmate in the endgame, without queens.

You have already seen many endgame checkmates in the chapter on checkmating patterns. You need to look for signs that checkmates are possible. One of these factors is the escape routes available to the enemy king. Another is the availability of access routes for the attack. These are naturally the main elements of any attack, but in the endgame, they are of supreme importance.

A New Queen is Crowned

The easiest way to win an endgame is to promote a pawn to a new queen. Normally, your opponent will do everything possible to stop you from promoting a pawn.

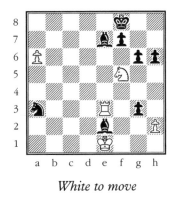

White to move

White can capture Black's bishops, knight, and two pawns. Yet it is pointless to do so. White simply pushes the pawn to a7, and Black can't prevent a new White queen from appearing in a position to attack Black's king. Remember, getting a new queen is as valuable as capturing all three of Black's pieces!

Escaping With a Draw

The stalemate is one way to escape a bad position. In the endgame there are many possibilities to set up a stalemate. However, you don't want to be in such a position, because it usually means you have no chance to win the game and are in a bad position.

Another possibility, far easier to accomplish, is to eliminate enough of the enemy force until it's too weak to force a checkmate. Even better, leave your opponent with so little force that there is no way you can be checkmated, even if you play foolishly. Remember, you must eliminate all pawns if you want to use this method of escaping to a draw.

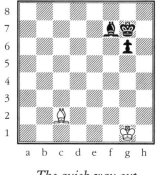

The quick way out

There is no plausible way for White to win this game. A draw is all that can be hoped for. The best move in this position is to capture the pawn at g6. After Black recaptures, the remaining bishop cannot checkmate White's king under any circumstances.

No checkmate possible

Even if the White king sits in a corner square of the same color as the one the bishop travels on, there is still no possible checkmate. The same would be true if Black has a knight instead of a bishop. So, if you have no chance of winning, head for a *no mating material* draw. These positions are drawn by rule, and can be claimed by either player.

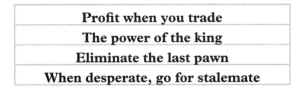

WHY KEEP PLAYING?

Some players get very upset when they blow a winning position, especially if they believe their opponent was behaving badly. So, in the position above, one player might want to play on just to be obnoxious. Because such things do happen in chess, it's nice to have a rule against such behavior.

Four Keys to the Endgame

As with the other stages of the game, it is possible to offer four simple guidelines to help find good moves. I should warn you, however, that endgames can be very tricky. There's a fine line between a draw and a win or loss, so you have to be very careful in the final stage of the game.

Profit when you trade
The power of the king
Eliminate the last pawn
When desperate, go for stalemate

Profit When you Trade!

Exchange pieces when you are ahead. By reducing the fighting force on each side, your advantage becomes more important. You want to hold onto your pawns, because they are your future queens. Try to keep one or two around, because it's much easier to win the game when you have an extra queen or two.

White can promote the pawn quickly

The easiest way to win this game is to exchange rooks, then promote the pawn to a new queen. You should already know how to checkmate with the queen when the enemy king has no helpers.

    1.Rc2xc7+   Kc8xc7

The pawn will march forward

There is no way for the Black king to catch White's pawn before it promotes. The pawn needs just three steps to reach the promotion square, but Black's king is five squares away.

The Power of the King

In an endgame, especially one without queens or rooks, it is usually safe for your king to take part in an attack. When your pawns march forward, your king belongs in front of your pawns, not behind them.

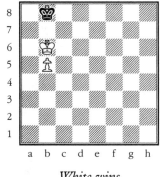

White wins

In this position, White wins by moving the king horizontally one square, and then advancing the pawn. Black has to try to keep White's king from reaching the "escort" squares a7 or c7. Once the king lands on one of those squares, there is no stopping the pawn.

1.Kb6-a6	**Kb8-a8**
2.b5-b6	**Ka8-b8**
3.b6-b7	

Black to move must lose

It is Black's move. The king must go to c7; it is the only legal move. Then White's king gets to a7 and escorts the pawn to the promotion square, b8.

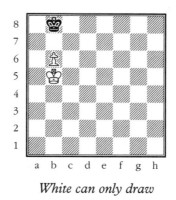

White can only draw

If we switch the position around so that the king is behind the pawn, Black can draw, thanks to the stalemate rule.

1.Kb5-a6	**Kb8-a8**
2.b6-b7+	**Ka8-b8**

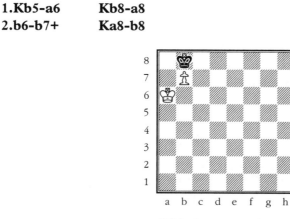

White has no good move!

If White moves the king to b6, Black is in stalemate. Any other move loses the pawn. That leads us to our next topic.

Eliminate the Last Pawn!

We saw this theme in the introduction. If the opponent has only one pawn left, get rid of it if you can.

Black's pawn looks unstoppable

Black is threatening to advance the pawn with check, and then take another step to become a queen. White can draw the game by capturing the pawn with the knight. Black will capture the knight, leaving the White king all alone. Bishop and king cannot checkmate a lone king, so there is nothing to worry about. White can claim the game as a draw.

When Desperate, Go for Stalemate.

If you have a lost game, get rid of the rest of your pieces so you might get stalemated. This is like the "Hail Mary" pass in American football, where the quarterback throws the ball down the field, even though all the defenders are out there. Whether the pass will be completed or intercepted is largely a matter of luck.

In chess, when a loss seems inevitable, you can sometimes escape with a draw by allowing all of your pieces to be captured or placed in positions where they cannot move. Then, if your king has no legal move, the game ends in stalemate.

Things look very bad …but!

As bad as things look, White can salvage a draw with a stalemate trick.

1.Qf1xd3+!   Kc4xd3

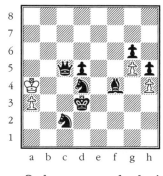

Stalemate saves the day!

The White king is in stalemate. The only available squares are covered by Black's queen and the knight at d4. White still has three pawns, but none of them has any legal moves available.

CHAPTER 9
The Sacrifice

We've already seen sacrifices in the opening, middlegame, and endgame. A sacrifice is not merely a tactic. The sacrifice is held in high esteem, and is considered part of the artistic side of the game. A sacrifice takes place when one side offers up one of his pieces, either for free or in return for a piece of lesser value. Queen sacrifices are admired most highly of all, but even the sacrifice of a mere pawn is well-respected.

There are two types of sacrifices: correct ones and mine.
—Mikhail Tal, 8th World Champion

Sacrifices are common, and we will see a few typical examples below.

A simple sacrifice

White can capture the pawn at h7, giving check to the enemy king. Black then has no choice but to accept, since the king cannot flee.

1. Qe4xh7+   Kh8xh7

Black accepts the sacrifice

Now the king can be attacked by the rook, by moving it to the h-file.

2. Re5-h5   checkmate

White checkmates Black

This is an example of Anastasia's Mate. The king is attacked, and cannot escape to g8 or g6 because of the knight at e7. White sacrificed a whole queen for a mere pawn, but the result is checkmate.

Let's take a look at a trickier example, but one that shows much greater artistry. Here is a spectacular example, surely one of the most familiar in the world. Many people would not immediately think of it, though, as it does not appear in many chess books.

THE HARRY POTTER SACRIFICE
COMPOSED BY JEREMY SILMAN

The sacrifice used in the chess game in the movie *Harry Potter and the Sorcerer's Stone* has been seen by millions. Its creator, International Master Jeremy Silman, worked with the writers to create a brilliant sacrifice that would involve the young characters in the film.

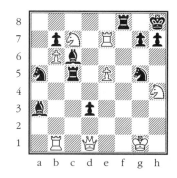

The position from **Harry Potter and the Sorcerer's Stone**

Harry and his friends are taking part in the game. Harry is the dark-square bishop sitting at a3. He'll eventually deliver the fatal blow. Ron, the knight at g5, is destined to sacrifice himself in the attack. Hermione, the rook at f8, will quietly contribute by staring down the f-file, prohibiting the king from fleeing in that direction. Two unnamed players, the rook at c3 and pawn at d3, will also give themselves up so that Harry can get the job done.

Things don't look too good for Black. Harry's team is missing its queen, though it does have two extra bishops and a couple of pawns. If the White queen can get into attacking position, Black's king could become the target of a formidable attack. So, Black has to keep the enemy queen busy while organizing an attack against White's king, who doesn't have any protectors.

1.Qd1xd3   Rc5-c3!

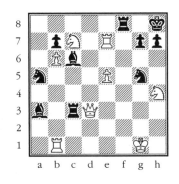

White has captured the pawn at d3 with the queen. In reply, the rook moves down from c5 to c3, attacking the White queen. The rook has no defenders, so this move offers a sacrifice. The point of the move is to free up a square at c5 so that it can be used later by Bishop Harry.

2. Qd3xc3   Ng5-h3+!

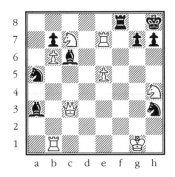

The queen gobbles up the rook at c3, only to spot Ron jumping from g5 to h3, giving check to the king. The game could have been brought to a conclusion more quickly if Harry had gone to c5 immediately to give check. Since the king would not be able to run away from the check, White would have had to capture Harry with the queen, and then Ron could have moved to h3 without being captured, resulting in checkmate. The producers wanted Harry to be the one to give checkmate, so this slightly inefficient sequence of moves was used.

3. Qc3xh3   Ba3-c5+

Ron is gone from the board and the queen enjoys another snack. But she has taken her eye off d5, and Harry slides in there to give check.

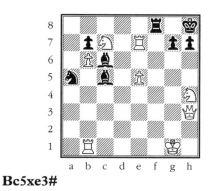

4.Qh3-e3   Bc5xe3#

There is nothing White can do except to have the queen block the check. She has no defenders, and Harry captures her with checkmate. Notice that at no time could the king escape. The f-file is controlled by Hermione from f8, while the bishop at c6 targets the h1 and g2 squares from afar.

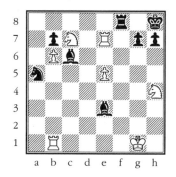

The complete tale of the creation of the positions is told at Silman's website (**www.jeremysilman.com**).

The Sicilian Offer You Can't Refuse

Sacrifices can be offered early in the game. Most of these are gambits, which we discussed earlier. Some sacrifices, however, take place rather later in the opening, just before the middlegame begins. Consider the position from the following popular opening strategy known as the Sicilian Dragon.

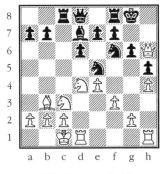

The Dragon's bite

In such positions, Black normally uses an *exchange sacrifice*, giving up the rook at c8 for the knight at c3. The idea is to weaken White's pawn structure and eliminate the powerful knight, which controls the important central squares c4 and d5. Here's an example from the opening known as the Sicilian Dragon, one of the fiercest openings of all.

14...   **Rc8xc3**
15.b2xc3

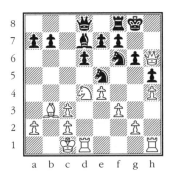

White has the advantage in balance of power, but the game will be decided by the attacks against the kings. White's pawn barrier is shattered, while Black's is still intact. Although hundreds of professional games have been played from this position, it still isn't clear which side has the advantage.

Don't Look Greek Gift in the Mouth

A sacrifice is even more likely in the middlegame, after the opening sequences have been played and the position is more familiar. The following sacrifice is so typical that it has a name: *Greek Gift*. The reference is to a Trojan horse, and is fitting because it is the knight who delivers the knockout punch, setting up a queen checkmate.

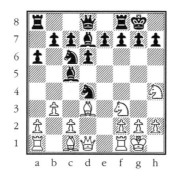

The position is ripe for a Greek Gift!

White sacrifices the bishop at h7 with a capture-check. This rips away one of the valuable defenders. If Black declines the sacrifice, White has at least won a pawn. Accepting the sacrifice is the true test, so let's see what happens if Black captures the bishop.

1.Bd3xh7+   Kxh7
2.Nf3-g5+

The knight comes into play

White checks the king with the knight, moving it to g5. Black can either advance or retreat.

2...   Kg8

If Black tries 2...Kh7-h6, then White plays a discovered check, 3.Ng5-e6+, and then takes Black's queen. Now White brings the queen into the attack, using the diagonal line opened when the knight left f3.

3.Qd1-h5   Rf8-e8

Black creates a flight square at f8

White threatened checkmate at f7, and moving the rook was the only way to create room for the king to move. Advancing the f-pawn would not have helped, because the knight covers f7 as well as h7.

4.Qh5-h7+   Kg8-f8

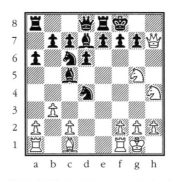

The king runs, but not far enough

5.Qh7-h8#

The Greek Gift sacrifice is not usually seen in such a pure form. Usually the king can also flee to g6, creating complications. In this example, the knight at h4 had that square covered.

Breakthrough in the Endgame

The endgame also provides opportunities for sacrifices. We have already seen examples earlier in this endgame section. Let's look at something a bit different. Here, the goal of the sacrifice is to promote a pawn.

BREAKTHROUGH REWARDED WITH PROMOTION

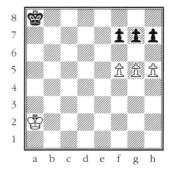

Break through the wall!

At first, it seems as though there is no way for the White pawns to get past their Black counterparts and reach the promotion square. The kings are far away and can't be of much help. In this position, they are irrelevant. Somehow, White must find a way to create a path for one of the pawns.

Each of the three pawns can advance, but only the center pawn will succeed, by moving forward immediately. If either of the other pawns moves forward, Black will exchange pawns and there will be no way to make progress.

1.g5-g6

The confrontation begins

Black must capture the pawn, since it attacks both the pawn at f7 and the one at h7. It really doesn't matter which pawn makes the capture.

1 ...   f7xg6

2. h5-h6!

Black's pawn at g7 is attacked

White does not recapture the pawn, but instead, advances on the flank to attack Black's pawn at g7. If White captures that pawn, a new queen awaits at the next turn. So, Black must capture the pawn at h6.

2 ...   hxg6

White has a clear path

3. f7-f6

The White pawn simply marches forward, and will turn into a queen in just two more moves, no matter what Black does. Sacrifices are very common in endgames, because giving up pawns or pieces for a new queen is a very good deal, indeed.

The Deep and True Sacrifice

A sacrifice is considered especially praiseworthy if the payoff is not seen for many moves. These long-term sacrifices are not fully calculated. They are so complicated that intuition plays as great a role as calculation. Here is a celebrated example, from the game known as "The Game of the Century," with the great Bobby Fischer playing Black.

THE "TRUE" SACRIFICE

DONALD BYRNE VS. BOBBY FISCHER
PLAYED IN NEW YORK CITY IN 1956

Black's queen is under attack

Fischer's queen is the target of White's bishop at c5. Fischer knew better than to retreat her automatically. After all, if she just runs away, the White queen will capture Black's knight, and Fischer would be a knight down. That knight is attacking the rook at d1 and is also covering e2, so it is quite valuable. There is always some compensation, because the White king at f1 cannot castle and is vulnerable at e2. On top of that, the rook in the corner is utterly useless.

17...   **Bg4-e6!!**

Who cares?

A truly stunning move! Fischer is sacrificing his mighty queen! In return for the queen, Black gets access to all the critical squares. In addition, the bishop at c4 will fall to a capture-check.

18.Bc5xb6   Be6xc4+

The bishop, which sat on the other side of the board just a few moves ago, is now directly attacking White's king. The king cannot step onto the e-file because that is owned by Black's rook at e8. So the king must slide to the right, trapping the rook in the corner. Since it's going to take a long time to activate that rook, Black's bishop and pawn are already sufficient compensation. Remember, Black is in check and the White bishop at b6 is under attack. So Fischer will collect that trophy, as well.

19.Kf1-g1   Nc3-e2+

Fischer is in no hurry to collect the bishop at b6. This knight cannot give checkmate, but it can inflict mortal damage.

20.Kg1-f1   Ne2xd4+

Using the windmill tactic, the knight collects the pawn at g4. Although the pawn doesn't seem to be of much significance, it turns out later that this diversion was well worth the time.

21.Kf1-g1   Nd4-e2+

The knight returns for the next stage of the windmill tactic.

22.Kg1-f1   Ne2-c3+

A windmill does not have to contain a capture with each discovered check. In this case, the knight gives the discovered check at c3, so it can capture the rook at d1.

235

23.Kf1-g1   a7xb6

Now Black has two pieces and two pawns for the queen, with the White queen and rook under attack, and the rook at h1 locked out of the game.

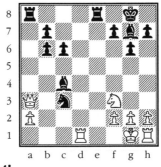

24.Qa3-b4   Ra8-a4!

Before capturing at d1, Fisher moves his rook to where it can attack White's queen, and indirectly protect the bishop at c4. The rook is guarded by the knight at c3, and the knight is guarded by the bishop at g7. So, White's queen can't capture any of the three pieces, and has to settle for a mere pawn.

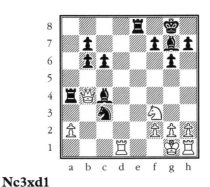

25.Qb4xb6   Nc3xd1

Fischer went on to win

Fischer didn't actually checkmate his opponent until the 41st move, but at this point he held the advantage of a rook, two bishops and a pawn against the White queen. On top of that, White's rook remains trapped in the corner, so victory was inevitable.

Here is a famous example by another great American player, Frank Marshall. It is said that when Marshall played his brilliant move, spectators threw gold coins on the board in admiration. Others say they were just paying off their wagers.

SHOWER OF GOLD

LEVITSKY VS. FRANK MARSHALL

The golden position

23...	Qc3-g3!!

Talk about "out of the frying pan and into the fire!" The queen, previously under attack at c3 from the rook at c5, moves to g3, where it is attacked simultaneously by two pawns and the enemy queen. White has to capture the queen, because otherwise, Marshall's queen will capture the pawn at h2, giving checkmate. White cannot capture the rook at h3 because the pawn at g2 is pinned by Black's queen.

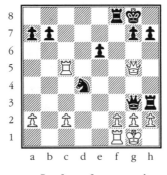

Look at the queens!

24.Qg5xg3   Nd4-e2+

Neither pawn capture would have worked. If White had captured with the pawn at h2, the h-file would be unavailable to White's king because of the rook at h3. So moving the knight to e2 would be checkmate. Capturing with the pawn from f2 doesn't have that particular problem, but notice that then Marshall would again have given check with the knight, and when the king moves to the corner square, Black's rook would sweep down the f-file and capture White's rook with checkmate.

A big fork from the knight

25.Kg1-h1   Ne2xg3+

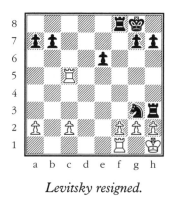

Levitsky resigned.

The knight cannot be captured by the pawn at h2 because it is pinned by the rook. If White captures the knight with the pawn from f2, Black's rook at f8 comes down and captures the White rook with checkmate. Of course, Levitsky could have played on by returning the king to g1. Then the knight returns to e2 with check, moving itself out of danger. After that, Marshall would simply have moved his rook from h3 to a3. Having an extra knight in the endgame would be an easy victory for such a skilled player, so there was no point in continuing.

All for the Sake of Art

Chess artistry is displayed not only in competition, but also in many other forms.

I am still a victim of chess. It has all the beauty of art—and much more. It cannot be commercialized. Chess is much purer than art in its social position.
—*Marcel Duchamp*

Chess is on a level with the other arts.
—*Alexander Alekhine,* 4th World Champion

Chess, first of all, is art.
—*Mikhail Tal,* 8th World Champion

Chess is the art of analysis.
—*Mikhail Botvinnik,* 6th World Champion

A chess game is a work of art between minds, which need to balance two sometimes disparate goals: to win, and to produce beauty.
—*Vasily Smyslov,* 7th World Champion

I like the last quote best, because it emphasizes one of the unique qualities of the game. Chess is collaborative art created by two adversaries, building on ideas developed over many centuries. Most artists actively work together toward a unified goal. In chess, they try to knock each other out! Let us not forget …

Chess is war over the board. The object is to crush the opponent's mind.
—*Bobby Fischer,* 11th World Champion

Chess is war; chess is all about testosterone-driven primal screams.
—*Garry Kasparov,* 13th World Champion

A more balanced view is perhaps needed, and another champion put it simply:

Chess is everything: art, science, and sport.
—*Anatoly Karpov,* 12th World Champion

Chess Puzzles

Chess puzzles with specific conditions are highly prized, while simpler puzzles drawn from actual games are found in newspapers throughout the world. Composers of fine chess problems are rewarded with honors and cash prizes.

In a chess puzzle, you are given a position and have to find a solution under the conditions set by the composer. In our example, one of the most ancient puzzles, White must deliver checkmate in two moves. Any other solution is unacceptable.

MATE IN TWO MOVES
BY "BONUS SOCIUS"
COMPOSED IN THE 14TH CENTURY

Finesse required!

With two rooks against a knight, White is bound to win sooner or later. However, arranging a checkmate in two moves isn't so simple! The knight is in a perfect position to block a check on the back rank. An immediate check is blocked, and then there is no checkmate.

1.Rh7–g7!

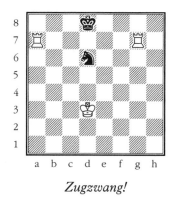

Zugzwang!

Only this quiet move will do! Black is in a squeeze. If the knight retreats and blocks one direction, the other rook will deliver the Rolling Rook checkmate. If the king moves in either direction, the rook on the same side as the king will complete the checkmate. Notice that if the rook were still at h7, Black would be able to prevent the two-move mate by moving the knight to f7, covering h8. The knight would be captured, but that would use up White's second move.

Endgame Studies

An *endgame study* involves more than just a puzzle. The solution must meet strict criteria. For example, there must be only a single solution. The solution must involve some clever trick, often a zugzwang. It is best if the first move not be a capture or check, because they are too obvious. The point of the puzzle is often to find the unusual. For example, promoting to a knight instead of a queen.

In an endgame study, it is best if the tricks are buried deep in the position, only to be exposed after many moves are played. Endgame studies are very difficult for all but the most knowledgeable players, who have likely seen the positions, or similar ones, before.

Invented Games

Another form of chess art is composed chess games. These are designed for maximum artistic value. Often the most interesting position is reached by a thoroughly implausible series of moves. In Alekhine vs. Grigoriyev (p.66), the great World Champion gets a bit carried away with promotion, producing a position with a total of five queens!

CHAPTER 10
Talk Like a Grandmaster

When you are around other chess players, you might sometimes feel a little bit intimidated by the use of fancy chess terminology and some unusual meanings for ordinary words. Don't worry; it's not very difficult to pass for a knowledgeable player, even if you don't have much experience with the game. There are numerous surefire ways to impress people (and an equal number of bloopers that will lead people to think of you as a chess ignoramus).

Let's consider, first, a few ordinary terms that have special meaning in chess. Then I'll give you some tips on how to impress people, based on a discussion I had at the 1990 World Championship match in New York City with New York Times reporter David Lewis, who used it in his front-page coverage. Finally, you'll be introduced to a few chess terms that are often mangled beyond recognition.

Exchanging One Meaning for Another

One of the most confusing terms in chess is "exchange." It can be used to describe simple trades of pieces or equal value, or of different values. "I traded my bishop for his knight." It also has a more technical use, referring to the exchange of a rook for a bishop or knight. "He dropped the exchange at f6." This disparity is often frustrating to those learning the game. Perhaps it would be better if we followed European tradition, and used the word "quality" instead. Perhaps not, though, since "I won the quality" sounds even worse than "I won the exchange!"

Where in the World is Kuala Lumpur?

When talking about very important chess events, often only the city is mentioned. It is assumed that a chess player familiar with major competitions knows which event is being discussed. Sometimes cities are famous for just one or two tournaments, especially when the event was chronicled in a classic chess book.

Chess players tend to know a lot more geography than the average person, because of the worldwide nature of the game. I present some of the most commonly mentioned locations, and their claim to fame. A whole book could be devoted to the topic, so this is just a selection of cities associated with a specific event or traditional event. I've tried to emphasize the more exotic ones.

Familiarity with these cities makes it easy to take part in conversation and impress folks. For example, if someone makes a reference to a tournament in Chalkidiki, you can show off by saying that the Greek food must have been a great treat. How many people would know that Chalkidiki is located in Greece?

The map below shows some of the cities that are indelibly marked as being associated with specific milestones in chess history.

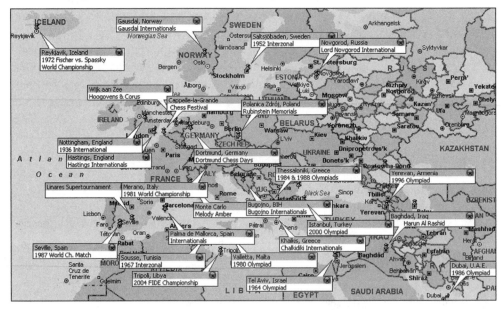

The major cities of the world play host to many of the most important chess tournaments. London and Moscow have held so many championship and other major events that they are known as major chess centers, not known for any one contest in particular. On the map you find competitions held in some surprising places. Each has earned a place in chess history.

When you mention Reykjavik, which has hosted many chess competitions, the famous 1972 World Championship match between Bobby Fischer and Boris Spassky immediately comes to mind. Merano evokes the fascinating 1981 title fight in northern Italy between Anatoly Karpov and Viktor Korchnoi, which formed the basis of the famous Tim Rice Musical *Chess*. Seville brings to mind Kasparov's title defense against Karpov in 1987, where the champion needed a last round knockout, and got it.

Famous steps on the path to the world championship were taken by Bobby Fischer at the 1967 Sousse Interzonal, where he walked out, and the great Palma de Mallorca qualifying tournament of 1970.

Chess Olympiads are generally referred to by location. For example, the "Valletta Olympiad" or, more commonly, "Malta Olympiad" is the 1980 event, #24 in the series. But if you mention "the 24th Olympiad," few people will know which one you mean, even though that's how it is often listed in reports and on websites. Among the cities organizing the massive event are Tel Aviv (1964), Dubai (1986), Yerevan (1996) and Istanbul (2000). Thessaloniki has organized two Olympiads, one in 1984 and the other in 1988, so "the Thessaloniki Olympiad" could refer to either one.

The current chess scene is dominated by talk of the supertournaments in Wijk aan Zee and Linares, held annually in January and February/March. Past supertournament series include the Novgorod and Bugojno events, which figure prominently in Garry Kasparov's career.

The professional circuit often includes annual competitions in Hastings, Cappelle-la-Grande, Dortmund, Gausdal, Monte Carlo, the Rubinstein Memorial in Polanica Zdrój, and Khalkis (Chalkidiki).

There are also cities that are famous for a single tournament, such as Saltsjöbaden, host to a famous world championship qualifier in 1952, or the great 1936 International in Nottingham. More recently, the FIDE World Championship Knockout in Tripoli added Libya to the list of famous chess countries. That event was possibly the greatest chess event in the Muslim world since Harun al Rashid's famous exploits in Baghdad over a thousand years ago!

In America, major cities have hosted all sorts of chess events, but a few special occasions have made the cities famous in the chess community. Las Vegas is known for the National Open and North American Open, while Philadelphia is the established base of the World Open.

New Kids on the Block

If you really want to sound like you know what you are talking about, you need to be familiar with some of the rising stars of the chess world. Let's meet some of the young players the chess world is talking about (ages as of mid-2006).

The top young players include Andrei Volokitin, 20, from Ukraine, as well as his countrymen 16-year-old Sergey Karjakin (holder of the record of youngest Grandmaster ever, at 12 years, 7 months) and Zahar Efimenko, also 20. Azerbaijan has a strong group of young stars led by Teimour Radjabov, 19, and Shakhriyar Mamedyarov, 20. Also making a big impression are David Navara (Czech Republic), P. Harikrishna and Humpy Koneru (India), Arkadij Naiditsch (Germany), Artyom Timofeyev (Russia), 17-year-old Hikaru Nakamura (USA), Ferenc Berkes (Hungary), Bu Xiangzhi (China), Evgeny Alekseyev, (Russia) and Ernesto Inarkiev, (Russia). All of them are grandmasters.

Hikaru Nakamura

The youngest grandmaster is 15-year-old Magnus Carlsen (Norway), followed by 17-year-olds David Baramidze (Germany) and Alejandro Ramirez from Costa Rica. 18-year old grandmasters Humpy Koneru (India) and Wang Xue (China) are the youngest female grandmasters.

It is a sign of the International nature of the game that these young stars come from such widespread countries and backgrounds.

CHAPTER 11
Chess in the Major Leagues

Chess is a serious profession for many players. People are surprised that it is possible to make a decent living playing this ancient game. Chess players have been able to earn millions of dollars in a single year. The big money comes in tournaments, but there is a fair living to be made in giving exhibitions, teaching, coaching, and even occasionally, some sponsorship. Of course, most top players have written books or made videos, as well.

Chess is only a recreation and not an occupation.
—*Vladimir Lenin*

For me chess is certainly more than a game—it is my profession.
—*Judit Polgar*

Let's take a look at some typical competitions that make up the tournament life of a chess star, and some other aspects of their lives. We'll examine the role of patrons and sponsors, how the press covers the game, team chess, drug testing, and other issues.

The Round Robin Tournament

In a round robin tournament, each player faces each other participant in one or more games. Round robin tournaments can have as few as four participants, or may involve dozens. Typically, there are ten to twelve players for a single round robin these days, and five to seven players if it is a double round robin, with two games against each opponent, one with each color.

In one of the most prominent chess news sites, TWIC, (*The Week in Chess*) discussed below), the results of a round robin tournament are reported as in the chart below. Because such charts are common in chess reporting, let's take a look at how they work.

```
---------------------------------------------------------------------
Smartfish Masters Drammen NOR (NOR), 27 xii 2004 - 5 i 2005cat. XIV (2600)
---------------------------------------------------------------------

                                     1 2 3 4 5 6 7 8 9 0
---------------------------------------------------------------------
 1. Shirov, Alexei         g ESP 2726  * = = = 1 1 = 1 0 1  6.0  2710
 2. Nielsen, Peter Heine   g DEN 2663  = * = 1 = 1 = = 1 =  6.0  2717
 3. McShane, Luke J        g ENG 2629  = = * = = 0 1 1 = 1  5.5  2676
 4. Lie, Kjetil A          m NOR 2474  = 0 = * 1 1 = = = 0  4.5  2613
 5. Korchnoi, Viktor       g SUI 2601  0 = = 0 * = = = 1 1  4.5  2599
 6. Macieja, Bartlomiej    g POL 2613  0 0 1 0 = * = = 1 1  4.5  2598
 7. Khalifman, Alexander   g RUS 2669  = = 0 = = = * = = =  4.0  2549
 8. Johannessen, Leif Erlend g NOR 2519 0 = 0 = = = = * 1 =  4.0  2565
 9. Carlsen, Magnus        g NOR 2581  1 0 = = 0 0 = 0 * =  3.0  2476
10. Stefanova, Antoaneta   g BUL 2523  0 = 0 1 0 0 = = = *  3.0  2483
---------------------------------------------------------------------
```

You can easily see that this is a computer-generated chart created with obviously ancient technology. Many web sites and books feature more attractive layouts, but you still need to be able to decipher the information. Usually the players are listed in their order of finish, with the winner at the top.

Here we have the Smartfish Masters, played in Drammen, Norway, from December 27, 2004 to January 5, 2005. It was a category XIV event, and the average rating of the players was 2600 on the Elo Scale. The winner was Alexei Shirov, a grandmaster from Spain (ESP) with a rating of 2726. He defeated (1) players 5, 6, 8, and 10; he lost (0) to teenage Grandmaster Magnus Carlsen from the host country, and drew (=) with the rest. The four wins and four draws added up to 6 points, and his performance was as predicted for a player rated 2710. As Shirov's own rating is 2726, and he was the top seed, he performed up to expectations.

The next three players performed much better than predicted by their ratings, so they will gain points on the next rating list. The bottom half of the field failed to perform up to their rankings, so they will lose points.

Let's take a look at a somewhat friendlier presentation, this time showing the results of the first supertournament of 2005, The Corus International, held in Wijk aan Zee, Holland. This chart includes world ranking, but not the rating information. The sequence of players in the chart was determined by lot at the beginning of the tournament. The initial order was used to determine who would play White and Black in each game, and the sequence in which the games would be played.

Name	1. Alexander Grischuk	2. Nigel Short	3. Alexander Morozevich	4. Luis Bruzon
Country	Russia	England	Russia	Cuba
Rank	13	29	6	47
1	—	½	0	½
2	½	—	0	1
3	1	1	—	1
4	½	0	0	—
5	½	0	½	0
6	½	½	1	½
7	½	1	1	1
8	½	0	½	0
9	0	½	½	½
10	1	½	0	½
11	½	½	½	½
12	½	0	½	½
13	½	½	0	½
15	½	½	0	0
Score	7	5.5	4.5	6.5
Place	4-7	12	13	8-10

Name	5. Veselin Topalov	6. Judit Polgar	7. Ivan Sokolov	8. Peter Leko
Country	Bulgaria	Hungary	Holland	Hungary
Rank	3	9	20	5
1	½	½	½	½
2	1	½	0	1
3	½	0	0	½
4	1	½	0	1
5	—	1	½	½
6	0	—	0	½
7	½	1	—	½
8	½	½	½	—
9	½	1	½	1
10	1	0	0	½
11	1	½	0	½
12	½	½	½	½
13	0	½	½	½
15	½	½	½	1
Score	7.5	7	3.5	8.5
Place	3	4-7	14	1

Name	9. Peter Svidler	10. Ruslan Ponomariov	11. Vladimir Kramnik	12. Loek van Wely
Country	Russia	Ukraine	Russia	Holland
Rank	8	16	4	24
1	1	0	½	½
2	½	½	½	1
3	½	1	½	½
4	½	½	½	½
5	½	0	0	½
6	0	1	½	½
7	½	1	1	½
8	0	½	½	½
9	—	½	1	0
10	½	—	½	½
11	0	½	—	½
12	1	½	½	—
13	½	½	½	½
15	½	0	½	½
Score	6	6.5	7	6.5
Place	11	8-10	4-7	8-10

Name	13. Michael Adams	14. Viswanathan Anand
Country	England	India
Rank	7	2
1	½	½
2	½	½
3	1	1
4	½	1
5	1	½
6	½	½
7	½	½
8	½	0
9	½	½
10	½	1
11	½	½
12	½	½
13	—	1
15	0	—
Score	7	8
Place	4-7	2

The Swiss System Tournament

The standard form of tournament is called a Swiss System. There is no elimination. Each round, players are paired with others who share the same score. After the first round, all the winners play another winner, losers are paired with losers, and those whose first game ended in a draw face each other. Weekend tournaments usually have 4-5 rounds, major national events consist of 6-7 rounds, and international tournaments are 9-11 rounds. One nice thing about this system is that when you lose, you usually face weaker competition, and it is easy to work your way back into contention. Pairings are usually made by computer these days. In the past, numerous errors were made by humans, and the errors were not always accidental!

#	1	2	3	4
Name	Stripunsky, A.	Nakamura, H.	Kaidanov, G.	Kudrin, S.
Rtg.	2533	2620	2611	2528
TPR	+219	+128	+31	+136
1	w 1/23	w 1/46	w 1/47	w 1/57
2	b 1/35	b 1/30	b ½/5	b 1/9
3	b ½/2	w ½/1	w 1/21	w 1/11
4	w 1/3	b 1/22	b 0/1	b ½/19
5	b ½/24	w ½/4	w 1/27	b ½/2
6	w 1/13	b ½/8	b 1/4	w 0/3
7	w ½/5	b 1/3	w 0/2	b 1/20
8	b ½/4	w ½/9	b ½/6	w ½/1
9	b 1/9	w 1/11	w 1/18	w ½/8
Score	7.0	7.0	6.0	6.0

#	5	6	7	8
Name	Shulman, Y.	Benjamin, J.	Onischuk, A.	Serper, G.
Rtg.	2549	2554	2653	2542
TPR	+85	+58	-67	+38
1	b 1/61	w ½/49	b 1/20	b ½/55
2	w ½/3	b ½/51	w ½/12	w 1/58
3	b ½/10	w 1/23	b ½/25	b ½/40
4	w 1/42	b 1/35	w 0/13	w 1/48
5	b ½/6	w ½/5	b 1/41	b 1/32
6	w 1/24	b ½/14	w ½/32	w ½/2
7	b ½/1	w ½/18	w 1/48	b ½/10
8	b ½/8	w ½/3	b ½/18	w ½/5
9	w ½/14	b 1/27	w 1/21	b ½/4
Score	6.0	6.0	6.0	6.0

#	9	10	11	12
Name	Goldin, A.	Gulko, B.	Ibragimov, I.	Becerra, J.
Rtg.	2620	2600	2585	2537
TPR	-45	-6	-7	+75
1	b 1/43	w 1/44	b 1/52	w 1/39
2	w 0/4	b ½/21	w 1/13	b ½/7
3	b ½/41	w ½/5	b 0/4	w 0/19
4	w 1/44	b ½/27	w ½/25	b 1/49
5	b ½/12	w 1/30	b 1/34	w ½/9
6	w 1/25	b ½/11	w ½/10	b 1/17
7	b 1/13	w ½/8	b ½/12	w ½/11
8	b ½/2	b ½/16	w 1/33	w ½/15
9	w 0/1	w ½/12	b 0/2	b ½/10
Score	5.5	5.5	5.5	5.5

#	13	14	15	16
Name	Fishbein, A.	Kamsky, G.	Akobian, V.	Wojtkiewicz, A.
Rtg.	2505	2717	2571	2539
TPR	+85	-159	-30	+13
1	w 1/42	b ½/50	w 1/37	w 1/38
2	b 0/11	w ½/32	b ½/29	b ½/19
3	w 1/51	b ½/44	w ½/18	w ½/48
4	b 1/7	w 1/29	b ½/30	b ½/33
5	w 1/19	b ½/16	w ½/21	w ½/14
6	b 0/1	w ½/6	b ½/40	b ½/23
7	w 0/9	b ½/33	w 1/32	b 1/36
8	b ½/26	w 1/22	b ½/12	w ½/10
9	w 1/32	b ½/5	w ½/16	b ½/15
Score	5.5	5.5	5.5	5.5

#	17	18	19	20
Name	Yermolinsky, A.	Gonzalez, R.	Novikov, I.	Milman, L.
Rtg.	2568	2428	2588	2434
TPR	-65	+133	-63	+40
1	b ½/40	w 1/54	b 1/41	w 0/7
2	w ½/50	b ½/28	w ½/16	b 0/42
3	b 1/52	b ½/15	b 1/12	w 1/54
4	w ½/34	w 0/24	w ½/4	b 1/38
5	b ½/25	w 1/37	b 0/13	w 1/28
6	w 0/12	b 1/19	w 0/18	b 1/26
7	b 1/44	b ½/6	b 1/50	w 0/4
8	w ½/20	w ½/7	w 0/27	b ½/17
9	w 1/23	b 0/3	b 1/33	b ½/25
Score	5.5	5.0	5.0	5.0

#	21	22	23	24
Name	Gurevich, D.	DeFirmian, N.	Bercys, S.	Shabalov, A.
Rtg.	2499	2550	2356	2608
TPR	+35	-32	+131	-135
1	b 1/56	w 1/33	b 0/1	w 0/48
2	w ½/10	b ½/48	w 1/62	b 1/63
3	b 0/3	w 1/29	b 0/6	w 1/37
4	w 1/45	w 0/2	w 1/53	b 1/18
5	b ½/15	b ½/40	b 1/50	w ½/1
6	w ½/22	b ½/21	w ½/16	b 0/5
7	b ½/24	w ½/23	b ½/22	w ½/21
8	w 1/40	b 0/14	w 1/24	b 0/23
9	b 0/7	w 1/41	b 0/17	w 1/43
Score	5.0	5.0	5.0	5.0

#	25	26	27	28
Name	Altounian, L.	Christiansen, L.	Perelshteyn, E.	Finegold, B.
Rtg.	2456	2531	2579	2531
TPR	+62	-69	-84	-84
1	w ½/63	b 1/36	b ½/58	b 1/45
2	b 1/49	w ½/34	w ½/55	w ½/18
3	w ½/7	b ½/32	b 1/36	b ½/34
4	b ½/11	w ½/40	w ½/10	w 0/32
5	w ½/17	b ½/33	b 0/3	b 0/20
6	b 0/9	w 0/20	w 1/43	w 1/42
7	w ½/29	b 1/46	w ½/40	b ½/41
8	b 1/48	w ½/13	b 1/19	w ½/43
9	w ½/20	w ½/29	w 0/6	b 1/46
Score	5.0	5.0	5.0	5.0

#	29	30	31	32
Name	Lapshun, Y.	Lakdawala, C.	Ivanov, A.	Schneider, D.
Rtg.	2461	2422	2582	2453
TPR	+12	+45	-170	+44
1	b 1/62	b 1/64	b ½/51	w 1/60
2	w ½/15	w 0/2	w 0/40	b ½/14
3	b 0/22	b 1/57	b 1/56	w ½/26
4	b 0/14	w ½/15	w ½/41	b 1/28
5	w ½/45	b 0/10	b ½/48	w 0/8
6	w 1/58	w ½/46	w 0/33	b ½/7
7	b ½/25	b ½/49	b 1/52	b 0/15
8	w 1/49	w ½/41	w ½/35	w 1/34
9	b ½/26	b 1/40	b 1/44	b 0/13
Score	5.0	5.0	5.0	4.5

#	33	34	35	36
Name	Lugo, B.	Browne, W.	Kriventsov, S.	*Goletiani, R. (w)*
Rtg.	2399	2455	2414	2336
TPR	+119	-34	-36	+85
1	b 0/22	w 1/59	b 1/53	w 0/26
2	w 1/53	b ½/26	w 0/1	b 1/60
3	b 1/50	w ½/28	b 1/55	w 0/27
4	w ½/16	b ½/17	w 0/6	w 1/47
5	w ½/26	w 0/11	b ½/42	b ½/43
6	b 1/31	b 0/48	w 0/36	b 1/35
7	w ½/14	w 1/38	w 1/61	w 0/16
8	b 0/11	b 0/32	b ½/31	b 0/37
9	w 0/19	w 1/45	w ½/37	w 1/48
Score	4.5	4.5	4.5	4.5

#	37	38	39
Name	Burnett, R.	Casella, M.	*Abrahamyan, T. (w)*
Rtg.	2444	2259	2238
TPR	-80	+62	+52
1	b 0/15	b 0/16	b 0/12
2	w 1/64	w 0/43	w 0/41
3	b 0/24	b 1/62	b 0/53
4	w 1/56	w 0/20	b 1/59
5	b 0/18	b ½/56	w 1/60
6	w 0/50	w 1/53	w ½/52
7	b 1/42	b 0/34	b 0/43
8	w 1/36	w 1/61	w 1/58
9	b ½/35	b 1/51	b 1/49
Score	4.5	4.5	4.5

The players are listed in order of finish, from top to bottom (though I've only included the players who achieved plus scores). There were ties for both the overall championship and for the women's title, so the players in italics were involved in head-to-head matches, won by 16-year old Hikaru Nakamura and Rusudan Goletiani.

#	Name	Rtg	1	2	3	4	5	6	7	8	9	Tot	TBrk[M]	TBrk[S]	TBrk[C]
1	GM Alex Stripunsky	2640	W19	W36	D2	W3	D23	W13	D5	D4	W9	7.0	41	50.5	36.5
2	GM Hikaru Nakamura	2676	W46	W29	D1	W24	D4	D7	W3	D9	W10	7.0	41	50	36
3	GM Gregory Kaidanov	2730	W47	D5	W22	L1	W26	W4	L2	D6	W18	6.0	42	51	31
4	GM Sergey Kudrin	2607	W57	W9	W10	D20	D2	L3	W21	D1	D7	6.0	42	50	34
5	GM Yury Shulman	2590	W61	D3	D11	W43	D6	W23	D1	D7	D14	6.0	41	47.5	32
6	GM Joel Benjamin	2620	D49	D51	W19	W36	D5	D14	D18	D3	W26	6.0	37	44	29.5
7	GM Gregory Serper	2598	D55	W58	D40	W48	W32	D2	D11	D5	D4	6.0	36.5	42.5	32
8	GM Alexander Onischuk	2680	W21	D12	D25	L13	W41	D32	W48	D18	W22	6.0	35.5	43	28.5
9	GM Alexander Goldin	2705	W42	L4	D41	W44	D12	W25	W13	D2	L1	5.5	40	48	29
10	GM Ildar Ibragimov	2671	W52	W13	L4	D25	W34	D11	D12	W33	L2	5.5	39	47	30.5
11	GM Boris Gulko	2705	W44	D22	D5	D26	W29	D10	D7	D16	D12	5.5	38.5	47.5	29.5
12	GM Julio Becerra	2582	W39	D8	L20	W49	D9	W17	D10	D15	D11	5.5	38.5	46.5	28.5
13	GM Alexander Fishbein	2575	W43	L10	W51	W8	W20	L1	L9	D27	W32	5.5	38.5	46	29
14	GM Gata Kamsky	2777	D50	D32	D44	W28	D16	D6	D33	W24	D5	5.5	36.5	44	26.5
15	GM Varuzhan Akobian	2665	W37	D28	D18	D29	W22	D40	W32	D12	D16	5.5	35.5	44	28.5
16	GM Aleks Wojtkiewicz	2590	W38	D20	D48	D33	D14	D19	W35	D11	D15	5.5	35.5	43.5	28.5
17	GM Alex Yermolinsky	2642	D40	D50	W52	D34	D25	L12	W44	D21	W19	5.5	33	40	26
18	IM Renier Gonzalez	2536	W54	D30	D15	L23	W37	W20	D6	D8	L3	5.0	38.5	46.5	28
19	Salvijus Bercys	2418	L1	W62	L6	W53	W50	D16	D24	W23	L17	5.0	37.5	43.5	24.5
20	GM Igor Novikov	2690	W41	D16	W12	D4	L13	L18	W50	L26	W33	5.0	37	44.5	27

Nakamura was slightly behind Stripunsky on tie-breaks, so he is listed second. His rating at the start of the event was 2620. In the next column, the +128 indicates that his performance was 128 points better than his rating, and this information could have been displayed by using a performance rating of 2748.

Next we see the round-by-round results. Nakamura started out playing with the White pieces (w) against the player who finished at number 46, Stephen Muhammad. Nakamura won (1) that game.

The Knockout Competition

In recent years the knockout format, used in the very first international tournament, has made a comeback. The knockout format has added a luck factor to the tournament competition, because a single bad move can lead to elimination. In most cases, the early rounds of a knockout have two-game matches. To win the match, you just need to win one game and draw the other. At the professional level, draws are very likely, so whoever wins the first game of the match has a great chance to move on.

Tied matches have playoffs, usually at a very fast time control. If even these matches are tied, some competitions resort to the Armageddon time control, described earlier. As in most sports, professionals find tiebreaks a rather disgusting way of settling the result, with luck playing a much greater role.

Name	Rtng	G1	G2	Rp1	Rp2	Bz1	Bz2	SD	Total
Round 4 Match 01									
Galliamova, Alisa (RUS)	2467	1	1						2
Khurtsidze, Nino (GEO)	2430	0	0						0
Round 4 Match 02									
Matveeva, Svetlana (RUS)	2428	½	1						1,5
Sebag, Marie (FRA)	2415	½	0						0,5
Round 4 Match 03									
Kovalevskaya, Ekaterina (RUS)	2458	½	½	0	½				1,5
Xu, Yuhua (CHN)	2502	½	½	1	½				2,5
Round 4 Match 04									
Chiburdanidze, Maia (GEO)	2511	1	0	0	0				1
Cmilyte, Viktorija (LTU)	2475	0	1	1	1				3

WWCC 2006

Patrons and Sponsors

As in music and other arts, major chess events and minor competitions alike have relied on the largess of wealthy individuals to provide opportunities for great chess to be played. A few decades ago, corporate sponsorship became available in much of the world. Following the collapse of communism, it became necessary to have real prize funds for chess competitions. The hundreds of professional chess players in communist lands lost their government support, which was their primary source of income. Fortunately, the prestige of the royal game encouraged many companies to sponsor national and international competitions. These include such familiar names as IBM and Pepsi.

Unfortunately, the United States did not benefit greatly from this sponsorship. The success of the great Bobby Fischer had a downside. Because Fischer was so difficult to do business with, and potential American sponsors would not think of funding an expensive event without him, expansion of international and professional chess was limited. There were plenty of offers, even without the participation of the man who was then the greatest player in the history of the game. I once was asked to pass one along a deal worth over $1 million from a prominent American television network. They wanted to host a great international tournament, but Bobby insisted that he would only participate in a match against a single opponent. That was unacceptable, because the network knew there was always the risk that he might not turn up for the event, and if it was a match, they would have no options that would be worth the money. They were willing to take the risk if it was a tournament, because they planned to have all of the world's top players participate, and if Fischer reconsidered abandoning his retirement, they would still have a stellar event. So no agreement was reached, and the event never took place.

Why should the United States have been left out, when American companies were funding tournaments in other countries? It seems that the corporate world considered Europe and other global destinations to be places where chess was held in high regard. They knew that their competitions would receive a tremendous amount of coverage in newspapers and on television.

There just isn't enough televised chess.
—David Letterman

In Europe, for example, news about chess was generally handled in the sports pages, but elevated to front-page news for superstar events. In European films and television, chess is presented in the context of dramatic intellectual warfare. In America, chess was generally used to indicate some sort of nerdiness, with scenes in school chess clubs and in parts, rather than the grand hotels and high society typical in Europe.

The Press

Famous chess journalist Dmitri Bjelica files three stories simultaneously.

Major chess events have always enjoyed a lot of attention from the media, though less so in the United States. A record 619 journalists from all over the world were accredited for the 1986 World Championship in London. That's not likely to be matched, since the Internet has made long-distance coverage easier and far less expensive. Television coverage of the title matches was common, though now, most matches are observed on the Internet. Nevertheless, the mainstream media often cover chess events at all levels of competition, from scholastic tournaments to the political comments of Garry Kasparov, who is a significant figure on the Russian political scene and writes commentary for the Wall Street Journal.

Pomp and Circumstance

Although American major chess events draw a few prominent businesspeople and a politician or two, in Europe it is not at all uncommon to see extremely prominent politicians, major sports stars, and other celebrities coming to watch the games, or at least turning up for the pageantry of the opening or closing ceremonies.

Indeed, the grand spectacles that accompany European events are often quite dazzling. One of the attractions is often a well-stocked hospitality suite, or champagne-filled party. Top chess players often lead very interesting lives, and you'd be surprised at how well developed their social skills are. The stereotype of the clueless nerd rarely applies to chess superstars. Unlike their athletic counterparts, chess players don't mind knocking back a few drinks, or more, even on the night before an important game. After all, most top events involve playing chess only in the afternoons and evenings. So, professional players are often considered good company on social occasions.

Some of the most memorable social occasions have taken place in London, a city that has extended a warm welcome to chess for well over a century. Just before the start of the 1993 World Championship match between Garry Kasparov and Nigel Short, a party was held at the Hippodrome. Everyone involved in the event was invited to join the cast of the hit "West End Musical Chess," written by Tim Rice. The cast not only got to meet some of the sorts of chess people they were portraying, but even met the man many consider to be the actual model for the important role of the arbiter in that musical. No, it wasn't me; it was the famous British arbiter and chess master, Stewart Reuben. They consulted him for tips, of course, but also chatted with many of us who could fill in some bits that Stewart himself might not bring up.

Perhaps the most impressive display of A-list celebrities took place at the 1986 World Championship match, also in London. Garry Kasparov was defending his title against his countryman, Anatoly Karpov. The first half of the match was held in London, with the second half in Leningrad, as St. Petersburg was then called. The opening ceremony was a black-and-white ball, a clever way of allowing everyone involved to fit in regardless of financial circumstances. There were plenty of tuxedos, but technically, a white T-shirt and black jeans would have sufficed. The star attraction was British Prime Minister Margaret Thatcher, though there were many other prominent politicians, both local and foreign. Hundreds of journalists covered the event.

Vladimir Kramnik, Andrzej Filipowicz and Eric Schiller at the
2000 World Championship

Team Chess

Although chess is primarily an individual sport, team chess plays an important role in the life of every professional player. Many players earn a large portion of their income competing for teams in various leagues, especially in Europe. There are also international team competitions, headed by the biggest chess event of all, the chess Olympiad.

In team competitions, the teams can face each other in team squads. However, there are also team prizes in individual competitions. The scores are calculated by adding up the points earned by individual team members. Generally, members of a team do not have to play against their teammates in a competition of this type, though rules and regulations vary widely.

Every two years, chess players from countries around the world gather in head-to-head competition in the chess Olympiad. Most national federations send a full complement of six men and four women, accompanied by coaches, trainers, and often a huge delegation of bureaucrats. Even when the world is afflicted by major international wars, chess players managed somehow to gather and compete for the highest international honor for their countries.

The chess Olympiad has been organized in countries all over the world, though the United States of America has yet to host such an event. It is an enormous undertaking, but even small nations such as Malta have welcomed the influx of the thousands of people associated with the event.

The best-known team competition is the hotly-contested German league, known as the Bundesliga. Even some of the best players in the world compete for the well-financed teams in that league. Teams are sponsored by various businesses. In American sports, outside sponsors get to put their names on the playing fields or stadiums. In the chess leagues, the team bears the name of the sponsoring organization. There are now team competitions in most major chess countries, except the United States, and some are elite, as in the Four Nations Chess League in Britain, while others are open to thousands of players, as in the German Bundesliga.

Team events are decided by adding up the points earned by the players, with various tiebreaking methods used to sort out the teams with equal scores.

Drug Testing

A few years ago, the World Chess Federation started implementing drug testing for certain competitions. They were not checking for recreational drug use, but for performance-enhancing substances. The chess-playing community was, for the most part, furious and uncooperative. The number one substance on the list was caffeine. Many competitors rely on large quantities of caffeine to keep our minds alert during the game. Professional chess players have investigated many common and uncommon substances, searching for anything that helps. Guarana and ginkgo biloba have been employed, as well as scientific regimens concerning blood sugar. Some players pointed out that if performance-enhancing substances were to be disallowed, players should not be allowed to consume any food during the game, and especially not chocolate bars or fruit, because of the energy they provide.

There is no known substance used by chess players to enhance performance that has been shown to be particularly damaging to health, and the only reason the drug testing was initiated was to satisfy the international Olympic Committee, which at the time was considering adding chess as an Olympic sport. A change in leadership at the IOC scuttled that idea, leaving the chess community with no reason to pursue such nonsense as drug testing.

In any case, many people think that professional chess players are not subject to the same kinds of drug testing that are imposed on athletes. In fact, they are subject to exactly the same restrictions: the international standard world anti-doping code. Some players are boycotting the events that enforce the code, and some arbiters, including your author, absolutely refuse to enforce them.

Major Events in the Major Leagues

Chess is not a seasonal activity. The life of a professional chess player is very complicated, because the international chess calendar is not always very well coordinated. Top players have obligations to teams, both national and commercial, and must always be prepared to alter a schedule in order to compete in the qualification stages for the world championships, which have been highly irregular and unpredictable in recent years.

The top players generally compete in highly selective tournaments. Although in the past, some of the strongest tournaments might have 16 or more participants, these days, for financial reasons, the number is usually 10 or fewer. The organizers are expected to provide not only hotel accommodation, but also travel money and an honorarium to the player, regardless of result. Price funds vary greatly, as you'll see in our little elite world tour, which will take you through a typical year.

Fortunately, many of the elite events have long traditions and tend to be held at a predictable time. Chess events are usually held off-season. Their organizers tend to look to hotels and resorts at a time when the best deals can be made on rooms, because accommodating the players is one of their greatest expenses. Although professionals like to compete in weekend events, top tournaments still tend to be about two weeks long. In the past, tournaments went on even longer; for example, when a tournament of 18 or 20 players competed in a round-robin. They were not going to play for over two weeks without any breaks, so the events often required three weeks.

Holding major chess events in the off-season also presents some challenges for the players, because the weather is often far from ideal. Few people would choose the Atlantic coast of Holland as a destination for a vacation in January. The little town of Wijk aan Zee plays host to an annual competition featuring many of the world's top players. The current sponsor is the Dutch firm, Corus, having inherited the event from its previous sponsors a few years back.

In 2005, the Corus Supertournament was won by Viswanathan Anand of India, generally known as "Vishy." He is one of the world's top players, and he battled Garry Kasparov for the World Championship in 1995. Kasparov won that contest, but he didn't compete at Corus and retired a month later. Anand won again in 2006, dominating the Kasparov-less field.

Narrow Escape

Vishy comes from the town of Chenai, on the coast of India. He was there when the 2004 tsunami struck. His house is on high ground, so he was safe, but he witnessed the devastation at close range, awakened by the noise of neighbors.

In addition to the top section, Corus also includes a number of other competitions, including opportunities for some of the top young players in the world to compete against established grandmaster competition. 2004 saw an amazing result when 13-year-old Magnus Carlsen of Denmark scored 10 1/2 out of 13 points. He is now one of the youngest male masters in the world.

The second major event of the year takes place in February, usually running into March, in the small, remote town of Linares, Spain. For a long time, Linares was the absolute top competition of the year, and it remains solidly in the top half-dozen. The 2005 event will be forever remembered as Garry Kasparov's final tournament, unless he chooses to come out of retirement. He easily won the event, and even a last-round loss didn't greatly affect his triumph.

One of the more unusual competitions takes place in spring in the casino city of Monte Carlo. Here the games are not played according to the traditional time controls of six or more hours per game. Instead, there are two competitions. In one, each player has five minutes to complete all moves. Since most chess games run about 60 moves or more, that means they have to make one move in an average of five seconds. This form of chess is known as "blitz." The other competition involves playing the games without sight of the board, known as "blindfold chess." The scores in each event are combined to determine the final standings. As this book was nearing completion in 2005, Vishy Anand was clobbering the field with a perfect score!

In summer, the calendar highlights usually include a unique man + machine competition, and a huge festival. In June, human players face off against each other in the Spanish city of Leon. The twist is that they may use computers to help them analyze the position. The players get great advice, but have to manage their time carefully.

The chess festival in Dortmund, Germany, is known as the Dortmund Chess Days. This event takes place in splendid surroundings, and features elite competitions as well as tournaments for the general public. The organizers work hard to attract the best players available.

The fall and early winter are usually devoted to various championship competitions, both national and international. In the United States, many states hold their annual championships on or near Labor Day weekend. The chess Olympiad is held in the fall.

CHAPTER 12
Chess in the Minor Leagues

Only the top-ranked players and a few young stars are invited to compete in the elite events. Most chess professionals earn their living by traveling on the open circuit. The competitions are open to all, and players generally have to pay their own way, sometimes even have to pay a fee to play in the tournament. When it comes to the open chess circuit, American tournaments tend to offer fewer incentives for titled players such as international masters and international grandmasters. Nevertheless, these tournaments often have attractive prize funds. The main difference between American tournaments and those held in the rest of the world is that in the United States, many prizes, generally more than half of the total prize fund, are reserved for low-ranked players.

Open chess tournaments are held in most of the countries of the world. The prizes and conditions are as varied as the cultures themselves. The vast majority of these tournaments are held on a weekend or over a five-day period. Sometimes all players compete in one section, but more often, players are divided into groups according to their rankings. Professionals play in the top section, of course.

To give you a picture of a typical chess itinerary is impossible. Some players are on the road all the time; others choose to participate in only a few events a year, spending the rest of their time teaching chess, perhaps, or training for tough competitions. To give you a taste of the exotic possibilities, I put together a tour of real events, the details taken from actual tournament announcements. No chess player has actually participated in this precise set of events, though some would if they had the time and resources.

The opportunity to travel is one of the great allures of the game of chess. Although the events presented here are professional competitions, in almost every case there is also an open event for amateurs taking place at the same time, often in the same room. So, if you wanted to, and had the time and money, you could actually follow a path like this and participate in all of these events right alongside some very strong players. Although the elite players don't often participate in open events, sometimes the organizers are willing to pay a considerable sum to have them come and play. Some fear losing ranking points, but many others like the idea of playing in an open event every once in a while.

We'll follow a fictional peripatetic chess player. I'll call him Mr. Bishop. Let's see what the first part of the year might look like for him.

Mr. Bishop decided to get a head start on the new year by heading for the traditional chess congress at Hastings, England, beginning on December 28. The event, which originated back in 1895, is one of the most celebrated chess tournaments in history, but it has slipped a bit, as funding has become a real challenge. The Hastings Borough Council, Eurotunnel, and other sponsors came up with the necessary funds.

In 2004 it took on a new format. Instead of placing top stars in a Premier section, relegating everyone else to the Challengers, all players compete in a knockout event. The losers don't have to go home, but will instead compete in a typical Swiss System. The quarterfinalists continue the knockout competition to determine the overall winner.

Although the weather was likely to be dreary, and it would mean celebrating New Years Eve in this British seaside town, Mr. Bishop knew that there would be a friendly crowd of players from Britain and many other countries. First prize was only 1500 British pounds (over $2500 US), but even if he failed to qualify for the quarterfinals, he could still pick up 800 pounds by winning the Swiss event. As long as he managed to finish in the top dozen overall, it should be enough to cover his day-to-day expenses. At least he wouldn't have to pay an entrance fee, thanks to his professional qualifications. And he could stay on for the weekend event following the tournament—a competition where he could likely earn another hundred pounds. So, he should plan to be in Hastings until January 10th.

"Mad Dog" Renman

Nils "Mad Dog" Renman is an international master and schoolteacher from Sweden, a real nice guy whose nickname comes not from an aggressive chess style, but from his ability to take on all sorts of challenges in a direct and uncompromising manner. He had been up at Gausdal, playing in the traditional Summer Open, which preceded the Berlin event, where many of us had also taken part. It was a bit surprising, then, to see him turn up in Berlin with a cast on his arm!

Renman related the story calmly, as if it were a tale of going out for a beer, or shopping. Seems he got on the wrong train, which was making an express journey in the opposite direction from Berlin. When the ticket-taker on the train explained this to him, Nils was flustered. How could he get to Berlin on time? If he remained on the train until the first stop, he could not catch the proper connections to arrive in Berlin on time. So he adopted a typical Mad Dog solution: he jumped off the speeding train—and broke his arm. Managed to get to Berlin in the end, though. Good thing Scandinavia has socialized medicine; in America it might have taken first prize just to cover the medical costs.

Night and Day

It is a little-known secret that three-time United States Champion Joel Benjamin, who helped prepare the Deep Blue computer that defeated World Champion Kasparov in 1997, doesn't travel too well. Some people easily adapt to new time zones and cuisines; some don't. Not that the problems are always Joel's fault —for example, when his second managed to forget to bring a passport. Sometimes, it seems that nature is at fault.

Our planet's 24 hour period is divided into day and night, with fairly obvious differences between the two. The presence of light in the former and stars in the latter are usually a dead giveaway. But two inventions screwed things up. First, Tom Edison gave us artificial light, so that adjourned positions could be studied. Earlier, some un-credited person invented curtains, so that adjourned positions could be studied in private.

Joel arrived at the 1984 Berlin Summer Open in his usual state of complete and utter jet-lag. Somehow managing the check-in procedure at the four-star hotel on Los Angeles Platz, he stumbled to his room, dropped down on the bed and fell asleep. I had arrived the previous day and was milling about the playing hall, checking out the participants and looking forward to seeing Joel among them. Sure enough, he was registered, and was expected to turn up for the 4 PM start of round 1.

Joel is a reliable and punctual chess player, so shortly after the start of the round I went to his board to say hello. No Joel. A few minutes later, still no sign of Joel. I checked at the front desk, and sure enough, they indicated he had arrived the previous night. I thought he might be ill, since he doesn't travel well, so I rang his room. A groggy voice answered. It was Joel's, and he didn't sound too happy. He asked me why I was calling at 4:30 in the morning. I explained that it was 4:30 in the afternoon, which came as quite a shock to him. He rushed downstairs, feeling not only un-refreshed (no time for a shower) but also guilty.

He had apparently responded sharply to the cleaning lady who had knocked on his door at what he thought was an ungodly night-time hour, but of course, she had just been making her normal morning rounds. Joel recovered to have a decent tournament and a pleasant time in Berlin, even though a Chess Life photo of a few years ago shows him climbing a wall ---- The Berlin Wall.

That leaves plenty of time to head to Prague for the annual open tournament from January 14 to 21. Mr. Bishop has plenty of friends in Prague, so he doesn't even need to pay for a place to stay. Even though the prizes are not particularly generous, this is a low-cost event and is not too much of a detour.

So the next question is, how to travel from Prague to Gibraltar to play in the Gibtele.com Masters International. No rush; he doesn't have to be there until the 23rd. He decides to stop on the way and visit some chess friends in Spain, and perhaps give a simultaneous exhibition to cover his expenses. After all, he wants to be well rested for this very strong open competition. The eight major prizes are topped off by the 4000-British-pound first prize (about $7500). It won't be easy to win this one, as at least one elite superstar will play, but Mr. Bishop is confident that he has a real shot at a good prize. Besides, it is a real high-class event with excellent playing conditions.

The tournament ends in early February, allowing almost a week to travel north to Cappelle La Grande in France. That massive festival will be quite a contrast to the rarified atmosphere of Gibraltar. Quite a bit colder, too. Over 500 players will compete for the first prize of 3000 euros (over $3000), but he'll probably be in the top dozen seeds. The competition ends in mid-February, giving him time to prepare one of his students for the big Commonwealth Championships.

This is one of Mr. Bishop's useful travel strategies. The Commonwealth Championships are scheduled for February 27 through March 3rd, in Rajasthan, India. That comes right before the start of a tournament in another Indian city, Raipur. His student's parents and other sponsors are paying for his trip to the Commonwealth, where he isn't eligible to compete. But the money earned from his coaching sessions, plus the free travel, covers the entire cost of his participation in Raipur!

The Chief Minister's International Open Chess Tournament in Raipur has a $12,000 prize fund, and the competition shouldn't be too tough. Of course, India is a chess power, and the local players will be tough. Still, no chance that Vishy Anand will turn up for that kind of money.

The Indian events finish up by March 20, and after all that work, Mr. Bishop decides to make a rest stop on the way to America, which has a dazzling lineup of big prize fund opens from April through July. Some of the events are held at casinos, so the actual prizes depend a lot on how much time is spent at the blackjack tables.

The first event is on the East Coast, at the Foxwoods Casino in Connecticut. Mr. Bishop decides to journey via Hawaii, as usual, because the chess community is very friendly there. He'll stay with friends, give a simultaneous exhibition or two, and take a break before traveling on to Minneapolis, Chicago, Las Vegas and Philadelphia for major open tournaments. At these events he'll have to play well, because almost all expenses come out of his own pocket. However, there are lots of prizes, so he shouldn't go home empty-handed.

The second half of the year would be more of the same, but would concentrate on European events and team play, where more income is guaranteed. The extensive travel isn't a problem, because frequent-flyer miles pile up quickly for a chess professional, and upgrades and free flights are frequently available.

CHAPTER 13
Chess for John Q. Public

You don't have to be a professional to enjoy many of the fringe benefits of playing competitive chess. Indeed, most competitive chess is open to amateur players. There is a huge, well organized scholastic chess community with competitions often featuring thousands of kids. In this chapter, we'll take a look at some of the programs for chess in schools, and look at some of the kinds of activities that are typically found there and in chess clubs. We'll zero in on two of the most famous chess clubs—one in San Francisco and one in London.

Chess in Schools

Ever since the discovery that playing chess leads to improved scores on standardized tests, schools have been scrambling to implement chess programs. Most of these programs are open to all students, but there are also chess programs restricted to talented and gifted children. Quality of the these programs varies enormously. Some school districts are fortunate enough to have titled masters providing the instruction, while other draft just about anyone familiar with the game.

To be honest, the quality of classroom chess instruction is not all that important. Once kids are exposed to the game, those who have the inclination and talent can find many ways to improve their game, a topic we'll cover a bit later. What's important is that the United States has finally, over the past two decades, allowed chess to play a more significant role in education. In some places, chess is even part of the mandatory curriculum.

World champion Garry Kasparov has long maintained that every child should receive chess instruction as part of one school year. He feels that a basic understanding of the rules and goals of the game will be helpful and useful as part of a general education.

There are a great many national and regional organizations involved with school chess programs. There are also foundations providing assistance in various ways. If you are interested in having chess made available in your local schools, you can turn to the United States Chess Federation for advice and pointers to appropriate organizations (**www.usches.org**).

Providing scholastic chess classes is a highly competitive business these days, so you are likely to have many options if you live in a major metropolitan area. If your school is located far away from any major chess center, qualified teachers may be in short supply, but instruction is also available on the Internet. That topic will be discussed later on in the final chapters of this book.

The goal of many American kids is to qualify for the squad selected to play at the World Youth Chess Championships. This event is usually held in an exotic and pleasant location, and it provides a chance to meet other kids who love chess.

U.S. Team at the 1998 Word Youth Championships
(the author, team coach, is the bearded one on the right; front row young stars are
Hikaru Nakamura, Vinay Bhat, Laura Ross and Matthew Ho)

Especially in Europe, chess events for children are well-funded and often have a lot of special activities that make the experience a great deal of fun. In the United States, such competitions are often located near major resorts such as Disney World, so there is plenty to do to keep the kids happy, (though the expenses can add up). Traveling to chess events provides children with a great opportunity to develop a broad perspective. Whether it is a tournament in a distant and unfamiliar region of the United States, or a foreign competition, it is usually a great learning experience as well as a lot of fun for the kids.

Most youth tournaments do not require any special qualifications, and are open to all kids. A number of my students have had the opportunity of competing in scholastic events in foreign countries, and they have always found it a wonderful experience. The young players get to meet kids from all over the world, and often make new friends. Because the youth events are subsidized in many countries, as opposed to the more profit-oriented American events, it often costs a lot less than you might think to travel to and participate in a foreign scholastic chess competition. If you are planning some family travel, you might well consider the possibilities offered by the international chess community. You can find most of these events listed at the World Chess Federation's web site.

♔ ♕ WEBSITE LINK

The World Chess Federation's web site is www.fide.com

Kids enjoy a unique chess cake.

Chess Clubs

The chess club was once thought of as a noble and dignified place, often restricted to adults, but the great chess explosion created by Bobby Fischer's success in 1972 opened up many clubs to an influx of younger and more diverse players. The Internet has had a major effect on membership. Since it is now possible to play a game of chess anytime, day or night, traveling to a weekly chess club is often no longer necessary. Recent years have seen the demise of some venerable institutions, including New York's Manhattan Chess Club, thereby ending the great rivalry with the Marshall Chess Club located downtown in Greenwich Village. Nevertheless, some chess clubs have grown and even prospered by offering a greater variety of activities to its members.

The Marshall itself is doing well, as are other clubs, including the oldest club in the nation, the Mechanics' Institute Chess Club in San Francisco. We will take a brief look at that club, and also a typical London pub club, where the atmosphere is quite a bit different from what one might expect to find at a chess club.

America's Oldest Club: Mechanics'

The Mechanics' Institute building houses the oldest chess club in the United States. It was organized in 1854, when San Francisco was a frontier community. The first meeting of the Mechanics' Institute was held on December 11, 1854, and April 24, 1855 is considered to be its incorporation and founding date. The early years of the Chess Room are not well documented, but chess was played during the Gold Rush. The great Pierre Saint-Amant, one of the top players in the world in the 1840s, was French Consul in San Francisco from 1851-52. It appears he left the Bay Area before the founding of the Mechanics', so the honors for the first world-class player to visit San Francisco go to Johannes Zukertort, who spent nearly a month in the City in July of 1884.

The 1906 earthquake destroyed the Mechanics' Institute, but it didn't take long for chess activity to spring up again. The Club erected a temporary building at Grove and Polk Streets, where it had bought a block of land in 1881, on which now stands the Civic Auditorium. The Institute's Office opened on May 23, 1906, construction was begun on June 4th, and after many trials, the new building opened its doors in August, about four months after the fire.

In the last century, the MI has hosted many world champions, including Lasker, Capablanca, Alekhine, Euwe, Fischer, Smyslov, Petrosian, Spassky and Karpov. The Club has access to the wonderful library, including a magnificent collection of chess books. There is so much chess activity at the Club, and so many chessboards to be seen on a nearby stretch of Market Street, that a major local bookstore (Stacey's) has greatly expanded its selection of chess books.

So if you are in San Francisco, just walk to the intersection of Post and Montgomery and Market streets, or take public transportation, and walk up to 57 Post Street to have a look at this venerable but vibrant institution. You'll find all sorts of players, from distinguished personalities of the business world to radical politicians from the streets. Chess brings everyone together in this most diverse of chess clubs. Their website is **www.chessclub.org**.

King's Head

On the other side of the world, there are similar venerable chess clubs, and wherever you travel, you'll find some place to welcome you with a game of chess. In London, there are many clubs. One of the friendliest is the King's Head Chess Club (**http://212.67.202.26/~khcc/start.shtml**). I played for them when I was living in London in the early 1980s. You might think that beer and chess are an odd combination, but in fact, chess clubs and tournaments have been sponsored by producers of beers, wines, spirits, and liqueurs. So the King's Head, originally located in the King's Head Pub in Bayswater, is a very comfortable home to the chess community.

Simultaneous Exhibitions

One common activity in schools and clubs is exhibitions, where a strong player faces off against numerous opponents. These are known as *simultaneous exhibitions*, or more commonly, *simuls*. The challengers are arranged in a square, rectangle or circle, and the master moves from board to board, making a move on each one. Players are not allowed to move until the master arrives, unless the exhibition uses chess clocks, which is rare.

Traditionally, the opponents may "pass" up to three times. This doesn't mean they can skip their move; only that the master moves on to the next game, and the opponent can think until the next circuit is completed. The pace of the game picks up after a while, since the number of games decreases each time a game ends. Finally, when only one or two games remain, the opponents must move very quickly, especially if their boards are physically near each other. On the other hand, the master can use as much time as he or she needs.

Matthew Ho, age 10, gives a simul at Farallone View Elementary in Montara, CA

All world champions, and indeed almost every top player, has given simuls. Capablanca was superb in simultaneous exhibitions. At Cleveland in 1922, he went undefeated, winning 102 games and drawing one.

Of course, there is always a real chance to defeat the distinguished master, since the challenger can concentrate fully on the game, and the master must deal with all the opponents. When I was young, I managed to defeat one of America's greatest players, Sammy Reshevsky, in such an exhibition, and I have earned draws with other United States champions. Some American kids have even earned a draw against Garry Kasparov!

Grandmaster Raymond Keene introduces Garry Kasparov

In one of the most unusual exhibitions, Garry Kasparov faced off against strong young challengers in London, pictured above, and a group of top young American stars via satellite.

Blindfold Simuls

An even tougher task for the master is playing simultaneous games without sight of the board, while the opponents see the board as usual. These *blindfold simuls* require enormous mental discipline. Joseph Henry Blackburne once announced mate in 16 moves during one of his blindfold simultaneous games. The late George Koltanowski of San Francisco was a specialist in this type of exhibition, and he played many brilliant and exciting games this way. Even in his nineties, he was eager to keep extending his record as the oldest master ever to meet such a challenge.

In a blindfold exhibition, the master remains seated and the opponent's moves are announced using chess notation. The master must keep track of all the games mentally—an enormous task! Hard enough for one game, but when Koltanowski set the world record in 1937, he faced 34 opponents, winning 24 games and drawing the other 10.

To make things even tougher, the games can be played with time limits. Reuben Fine, one of American's great players, managed to play four games at once, with the stipulation that he could take no more than ten seconds per move!

George Koltanowski (seated right) sets a world record in Edinburgh

Postal Chess

Chess is still played by mail, though these days, email is the preferred form for most players, since it is much less expensive. But for persons without Internet access, sending moves by post is still popular. There are some benefits to the old-fashioned system, especially for those who like to collect stamps.

In correspondence chess, you can smoke during the game.
—*John C. Knudsen*

The International Correspondence Chess Federation (**www.iccf.com**) holds many postal and email competitions, from the Correspondence World Championship and Olympiads to informal events featuring specific opening strategies. They also award ratings and titles.

♚ ♛ CRAZY FOR CHESS

The inmates of the Bedlam insane asylum played chess, and even defeated prestigious Cambridge University in a postal game.

CHAPTER 14

How to Behave

Chess players everywhere observe some rules of conduct that are traditional courtesies. We shake hands at the start of a game, and shake hands again when it is over. This is the proper way for the loser to congratulate the winner, and the winner responds graciously. It never feels good to lose, but we all do so occasionally, and it is rude to display your disappointment by crying or carrying on, or any such emotional outburst. Likewise, winning might make you want to burst with joy, but don't celebrate in front of the player you just defeated, because that is rude.

Keep quiet while chess games are going on. Chess is not designed to be noisy. In casual play you are allowed to say "check" when you place the enemy king in check. There is no rule that says you must, but it's still a good idea, since you can't take your opponent's king if he doesn't get out of check, anyway. You must not do this if formal competition, however. You must speak only when you offer or accept a draw, or resign. If you say "check" in an event where the games are rated, the arbiter will likely give you a warning.

It used to be customary to declare that checkmate is forced. The player of the superior side would often stand up and declare, "Checkmate in [number] moves!" That is no longer considered good form, and in formal competitions it is improper. In casual play, it isn't a major transgression, but before announcing checkmate, you'd better check every possible reply. It will be very embarrassing if you are wrong. And if your opponent announces checkmate, don't take his or her word for it!

... a well-known player made a queen's move of decisive character. His
opponent studied the position for some time, and then said
"That threatens mate."
"Yes, señor, in three moves."
"Then why didn't you announce it?"
"Because I didn't see it!"
—*British Chess Magazine (1920)*

If you are going to offer a draw during a timed game, make sure you offer it after making your move but before you push the button on your clock. And if your draw offer is turned down for any reason, don't offer again for a long time. Repeated draw offers only annoy your opponent.

If your opponent has offered a draw and you want to keep playing, simply say so. You can also decline the offer by making a move, but it's better manners to respond verbally. Also, don't try to get cute by being sarcastic. One player had an easily winning position, with several extra queens and a few extra pieces, and thought his opponent should resign, so he sarcastically offered a draw. His opponent naturally accepted, and the tournament director ruled the game a draw.

Never ask your opponent to resign. You win by checkmate or when your opponent gives up, not before. The way to encourage a losing player to resign is to play your best moves. The proper way to resign, or give up, when you see that you're going to get checkmated, is to either say "I resign," or tip over your king. And don't forget to offer your hand. When should you resign? Beginners are usually advised to never resign. After all, the opponent can always make a mistake! As you get better, you'll find that opponents get a bit annoyed if you play on when you have an utterly hopeless position.

At more advanced levels, I think resignation is justified when you are convinced there is no way you can survive, even if your opponent plays very badly, and when all of the spectators would understand why you resigned. The last thing I want to hear when trying to get out the door after a loss is, "What happened? Why did you resign?"

There is no reason to resign in an endgame unless you cannot stop your opponent from obtaining an overwhelming advantage, such as a new queen. There are many tricky draws in the endgame, and the endgame is usually a player's weakest area.

When the game is over, it's a good idea to ask your opponent to go over the game with you, particularly if you've lost. That's the best way to find out what mistakes you made so you can avoid them in the future. If you have won the game, you should always invite your opponent to review it with you, unless the next round is coming up and you need a meal. The analysis should take place in another room, usually known as the *skittles room*. One of the greatest annoyances during a tournament is for nearby players to noisily analyze their game while others are still playing.

Another bit of etiquette that is very important to remember is the proper use of the word *j'adoube* if you don't recall how it is used. It is definitely not meant to mean "I want to take back my move because it is bad." J'adoube is only meant for adjusting a piece, as when you inadvertently brushed a piece on the way to moving something else. The touch-move rule is always strictly enforced in tournaments, and it is a good idea to get into good habits from the start.

Jadoubevich

In serious play, you aren't allowed to take back a move; it is considered outright cheating. Some players have used a belated "J'adoube" to try to correct a mistake. An infamous example took place in the World Championship qualifier in Tunis in 1967. Milan Matulovic earned the name "Jadoubevich" when he made a move, released the piece, but then said, mixing languages, "Ich spreche J'adoube." Then he moved the piece back to its original square and moved another piece instead. There was an appeal, but justice was not served.

The touch-move rule allows you to choose a different destination for your piece, if you haven't let go of it. In modern tournaments, the arbiters can go to the videotape. An instant replay in a game involving World Champion Kasparov was used in a case where some thought he had released a piece, but the replay was, as they say, "inconclusive."

Professional Appearance

Chess professionals are expected to dress properly for competition. Attire in suit and tie is generally preferred, though as the game progresses, the tie may get looser, sometimes disappearing entirely, and it is not unusual to find the players taking off their jacket, as well. However, in open tournaments the standards of attire are quite a bit lower, and in many cases there are none at all. Well, almost none.

Naturally the sponsors want to make the best impression possible, but open competitions, at least in the United States, rarely have such sponsors. Even in the most important open competitions, it is not unusual to see professionals attired in T-shirts and jeans. I've seen players barefoot at some of these events. The top players generally dress well at all times to create a good impression on the public, but many other professionals have a simple policy: If they are being paid an honorarium, also known as an appearance fee, to participate in the event, they will dress up. Otherwise, they will wear the clothes that allow them to be most comfortable during the game. Sitting for five or six hours in an over-air-conditioned room, or sweltering in a room with hundreds of people and no air conditioning, requires players to be prepared for just about anything.

As a teenager, Gary Kasparov used to wear a very intimidating leather jacket, enhancing his fearsome appearance as he paced around the stage. When he reached the world championship semifinals, he suddenly turned up in a suit. It seems that his mother had laid down the law, and I never saw the black leather jacket again. At one point, when Kasparov was struggling in the match, I even suggested that perhaps he needed to get back to his old attire. He didn't, but he won the match anyway. Since then, he has been very careful about his appearance when participating in competition, but informally, he is comfortable in jeans.

Chess players are often portrayed as large, bearded fellows, and even Bobby Fischer eventually let his facial hair grow out. Some players, though, are superstitious. Kasparov stopped shaving after playing bad moves for some time. However, these days, most of the top players are clean-shaven, except when they have early morning games, because turning up on time for an early morning match still presents a major challenge to many players who are accustomed to the traditional afternoon start time.

Grandmaster Abramovich

Short's Shorts

At the 1985 World Championship qualifying tournament in Switzerland, a heat wave combined with poor air-conditioning in the playing hall to create a very uncomfortable situation. The usually well-dressed British star, Nigel Short, decided to live up to his name by wearing shorts during the competition. This infuriated officials of the World Chess Federation, who have long worked to improve the sartorial standards for top professionals. Speaking with many of the top competitors there, I found out that quite a large number of them agreed with what Nigel did, but simply didn't have the guts to do it.

Spectators

You might find it surprising that the game of chess generally attracts a large crowd of on-lookers at all important events. World championship competitions sell out even very large theaters. Many spectators follow the play on their own pocket-sized chess sets. In most competitions, there are barriers separating them from the players, but front-row seats are often quite close to the play. In championship events, spectators are not allowed in the front rows because they might display their pocket sets or otherwise transmit information to the players.

Spectators must remain silent and not interfere with the games. Normally, people watching chess games are reasonably well behaved, though a big electronic "SILENCE" sign needs to be lighted frequently during championship competition to remind them to quiet down. When young players compete, it is not the uninvolved spectator who gets out of line; it is usually a parent! Chess parents are a lot like mothers of musical prodigies, and young stars in dance and sports; when they get carried away, they can do some crazy things!

♟ ♕ SUBMITTED FOR YOUR CONSIDERATION

A translation of the entire text of the book *Advice to Spectators at Chess Tournaments*: "Keep your mouth shut!"

Don't speak with the player except in the presence of an arbiter. Any violation of this rule may result in forfeiture of the player.

Do not point out time forfeits or other rule infractions, except to the arbiter, and even then, don't let the players hear you.

Photography is generally restricted to the first five minutes of play.

Display boards at the 1982 Bugojno Supertournament.
Borislav Ivkov (foreground), Garry Kasparov and Robert Huebner in back.

Chess games at major tournaments have always been displayed to the public. Before the advent of digital technology, huge wooden boards were used, and tournament staff would use long poles or even climb on ladders to make the moves. Nowadays, the displays are electronic, and in most cases the moves are transmitted directly from a digital chessboard used by the players to the video and Internet transmission.

Spectators seated in the audience can use small pocket chess sets to analyze the positions, provided that they are not in areas where such activity might be seen by the players. There are special rooms for analysis, but access is often limited to grandmasters and journalists.

In the heat of the fray, under the strain if an oncoming sacrificial combination or a winning rook and pawn ending, the master may express his
grief, chagrin, joy, hope or despair, according to his temperament and his
position. This is a helpful clue to the spectators, because often they can
glance over a tournament room and tell just whose game is in its
last throes.
—*Paul Hugo Little*

It is now possible to watch the games of most major chess events live, without
leaving the comfort of your home or office. Internet broadcasts of the games take
place on dedicated web sites, and also are relayed to many online chess clubs. I will
return to that topic a bit later on in the book.

"Kibitzing" is offering unsolicited advice during a game or post-game analysis.
During a tournament game it is against the rules. A player who receives advice can
be forfeited by the arbiter. Persons approaching a player during a game and offering a comment on it usually get cut off quickly by the participant to avoid getting
into trouble.

Chess Master Maurice Giles (left) conducts a post-mortem.

During a post-mortem, kibitzing may or may not be welcomed by the players.
If you see some important tactic in the game and want to offer advice, it is best
to wait until invited to join in. Most people can't resist jumping in, so if you are
conducting a post-mortem and don't want kibitzers, do it in private, or politely ask

onlookers to leave. The latter rarely happens though, because a post-mortem is an attempt to find the truth, and sometimes dispassionate onlookers can contribute to the discussion.

Press room analysis at the 1983 World Championship Semifinals in London. Legendary Grandmaster Miguel Najdorf holds court with the author and Russian journalist Alexander Roshal.

Many times, outside analysts can shed more light on the game than the players themselves. You don't always appreciate this as you listen in, because the players will often respond to a long, tactical variation by implying that they had, of course, considered that plan. Often, this is just a little white lie. No one wants to admit overlooking a tactic!

If you are lucky enough to be granted permission to visit the analysis room, a wonderful treat awaits. Grandmasters, and often other participants who have completed their games, sit around and argue about what is going on in the game. It is reassuring to see that a large group of grandmasters will rarely agree on the evaluation of the position, unless it is absolutely indisputable. The analysis room was a lot more fun before strong chess-playing computers came along. Now a grandmaster argues not so much with fellow chess players, as with computers. Fortunately, the machines still get a lot of the positions wrong, and there is always great satisfaction when a human chess player comes up with the better analysis.

Finally, here's some advice about watching games online at a chess server, where hundreds, and sometimes thousands of people are watching with the capability of posting commentary. This situation can be very instructive and a lot of fun. However, there are always several trolls around, who insist on discussing topics unrelated to the game they're watching, or to chess in general. At the Internet Chess Club, there is even an expression, "Fischer talk," for describing posts that try to change the topic of conversation to the controversial World Champion. In addition, you'll find that some people take the opportunity to insult players and other chess celebrities.

When you watch a game online, you're not in the same physical location as the people who are making these posts. They are spared any confrontation, though many hope you will rise to debate and give their remarks additional prominence. The best rule is to only make comments that you'd like to see made on one of your own games. Many people choose only to view comments made by Grandmasters and other titled players, and that's often a good option because their comments tend to be relevant, and at least indicate some mastery of the game. You'll also see a lot of computer-generated commentary, though some sites try to keep that in a separate chat room or channel. Since there is some ego reward that comes with being the first person to point out the correct strategy in a position, many people use their chess analysis programs and very quickly post that analysis, often not mentioning that it came from a computer. The problem is that computers take time to analyze a position and require at least a few minutes to present trustworthy analysis. A few seconds is usually insufficient.

Don't be intimidated. If you have a question about a chess position or move in the game, go ahead and ask. A lot of the spectators are just beginners, and they probably have the same question. The better commentators will always stop to explain advanced chess comments, though often, one of the other spectators will beat them to it. There is no reason to feel embarrassed when a move you suggest is quickly refuted by more experienced players. Remember, they were once beginners like you, and probably would have made the same suggestion, back then. Even with all the chatter and snide remarks, watching a game with online commentary and discussion can be one of the best ways of learning more about how to play chess well.

The major world chess events are covered live on at least one chess server, and often at numerous sites. Over time, I think we'll see a lot more specialized sites for different levels of players. Until then, simply explore a few and see where you are most comfortable. I've been referring mostly to the Internet Chess Club (**www.chessclub.com**), because it is the most established site and usually has the largest audience. There are many alternatives, however, and their interfaces and overall experience can be quite different. If you want to get the most out of watching top chess competitions live, you'll need to find a site with commentary that best fits your level, and offers an atmosphere you find pleasant and easy to navigate.

CHAPTER 15
Tools of the Trade

To participate in most hobbies, there are always certain items you just can't do without. In chess, all you need is a chess set, a chess board, and perhaps a chess clock if you want to play quick games. That's all you need to get started, but to make rapid progress in the game, you'll want to add some computer software (assuming you have a computer) and at least a few books. So we will take a look at a few of the options.

Chess Equipment

You don't need a particularly expensive chess set, but do get one with standard pieces that are durable and large enough so that they can be moved with natural arm movements. Chess sets are generally classified by the size of the king. Anything over 3 inches tall should be sufficient. Wood or heavy plastic are normally best.

The chessboard should have clearly contrasting squares, and be large enough so that the pieces are not squeezed together when you set up the starting position. Chessboards can be made out of almost any hard substance. Plastic boards can be rolled up for easy transportation, and that's what most tournament players use, though they usually have a fancier wooden board at home.

Buying a Chess Clock

Chess clocks are divided into two categories: analog and digital. An analog clock displays the time on a traditional clock face, and can only be set for a simple time control with a fixed period of time. I honestly don't know why anyone would consider going analog these days, as digital alternatives are available, often at a much lower price. A digital chess clock is a battery-powered electronic device that displays a digital readout of the time remaining, as well as some other information. But not every digital clock can be set for all of the modern time controls, some of which are quite recent innovations, so it is very important, before buying one, to scan chess magazines or explore the web for reviews that list the features included, and point out when a desirable feature has been left out. Having a lot of features means that most of the clocks approved for tournament use are rather complex and not all that easy to use. You'll likely need to spend some time with the manual.

If you intend to purchase a chess clock, be sure to get one that is digital and includes a wide variety of time controls. I recommend clocks by Saitek, DGT, and Chronos, though new additions are arriving all the time.

You may also want to pick up a booklet of blank score sheets for recording your own games. Score sheets are generally provided at tournaments, even at events for beginners, because recording the moves is required for rated games. Even if you are just playing an unofficial, unrated game, you might want to write down your moves. Then you'll be able to study the game later to learn from your mistakes, or have something to show off to your friends, or perhaps both.

Chess and Computers

Computers play a big role on the contemporary chess scene. Chess-playing programs have gotten so strong that they can even defeat the world's best humans, on occasion. There are programs you can play against, programs that will analyze your games and suggest improvements, and a wide range of instructional software. You can purchase CDs with millions of chess games on them, and programs that will analyze and present all that data in an easy-to-digest form.

Chess-playing Software

For under $50 you can purchase a full-featured chess program that plays chess well enough to defeat grandmasters frequently. The programs offer different features and interfaces, and often have ways of scaling back the power of the beast so that an average player can win once in a while. Although software package advertising tends to emphasize how well the program can play, for most of you that will be the least important factor. They are all strong enough to take you down every time.

Getting clobbered by a computer chess program is not particularly fun. If you are going to challenge a software program, you want it to play as much like a human being as possible, and that means making a mistake at least once in a while, as all human players do. It is very difficult to create a computer chess program that makes human-like mistakes; it is much easier to simply improve the program to play better chess. Many commercial programs boast that they offer all sorts of levels and styles of play, but the famous Turing test still applies. A great intellectual prize awaits the programmer and team who can fool experienced human chess players into thinking they are playing against another human being.

So, the best chess program to play against is one you can beat occasionally or frequently, if you are so inclined. If the experience is realistic and you enjoy it, then that's the right program for you. All of the major programs include useful instructional materials and bonus features, but be prepared to spend a lot of time sitting down and playing against a computer program, concentrate on that experience.

If you plan to use your chess-playing program to analyze games, you'll find that some programs offer a variety of commentaries, some even in English. Though the automated commentary gets repetitive, and sometimes can be quite irrelevant, it can be interesting to see how the computer reacts to the moves you make. You can have some fun comparing these commentaries with those in classic books. Not infrequently, the machine will spot significant flaws in the grandmaster analysis published in books written before computers learned to play the game well.

It really is a lot more fun to play chess against fellow human beings, whether in person or over the Internet. Eventually, we may see innovative programs that provide humanlike virtual opponents, but were still a long way from that.

Chess Analysis Software

Sometimes it seems that there is just too much data out there. There are already more than 4,000,000 games available for study. If you steadfastly studied a game a day, it would take 10,000 years to study them all. Even if you sped through a hundred games a day, just casually replaying the games, you'd need a century. Of course, games continue to be recorded at a frenetic pace. All of the millions of games played online are stored on the Internet, as well as are all professional and many amateur tournaments.

Chess processors are programs designed to ease the task of sorting through the pile of data. Chess Assistant (**www.chessassistant.com**) and ChessBase (**www.chessbase.com**) are the best-known, putting the power of the information age at your disposal, and allowing you to search for games according to almost any criteria you can imagine. They can search for players, tournaments, opening strategies and specific positions, delivering both the chess games for replay and a host of statistical analysis. You can even specify such criteria as: Show me all the games played by top players where a knight traveled to each of the four corners of the board, or, Find all games by world champions where the winner's army occupied each square of the chessboard at some point.

Chess Instruction Software

There are hundreds of software packages designed to improve your play. Major chess-playing programs often include elaborate tutorials. More intensive and specialized training is available if you have a serious interest in becoming a strong chess player. There are courses for all levels of play. Most include extensive testing, which can also be used to approximate your chess ranking on the Elo scale. Generally, you are presented with a position and have to find the best move. If you answer incorrectly, you are given a subtle hint and can try again.

You might think that this is a form of drudgery, homework of a sort that shouldn't be part of a game. In fact, many programs are designed to be highly entertaining. In any case, my school classes love to tackle the puzzles, working through the skill levels as if they were playing a regular computer game.

Playing Chess Online

One of the best ways to improve your game is to practice and play chess at an online chess site. There are numerous sites featuring online chess play, and they come and go. As I mentioned before, the oldest and most established of these is the Internet Chess Club at **www.chessclub.com**. Its membership spans the entire globe, and that means that you can find a game at any hour, day or night. They also broadcast live transmission and commentary of most of the world's major chess competitions. At this site and others, there are additional advantages for the student of the game. All of the moves of the game are recorded and can be replayed or e-mailed to you or to a chess instructor for evaluation. You'll receive one or more chess rankings, depending on the time controls you choose in your games. You'll even see a ranking that shows how you stack up against the competition.

At other online competition sites, you don't have to sit down and play a whole game. Instead, you log on and make your move, and when the opponents come online, they will see that you have moved, and make their reply. Then next time you log on, you will continue the game. Of course, these games can take quite a long time to play; they are more convenient for people with busy schedules. An example of this sort of site, aimed primarily at young players, is Academic Chess (**www.chess.ac**). That site has parental controls available to help protect kids.

There are dozens of places to play chess on the Internet, and if you're just getting started in the game it really doesn't make a whole lot of difference where you play. The more chess you play, the more quickly you'll advance and build important skills. If you are interested in watching top players compete, a major site such as the Internet Chess Club is the place to go, because that's where the grandmasters and professionals hang out.

Because the computer records the moves for you, you don't even have to know chess notation to play. You just point and click to move the pieces. Don't worry if you haven't quite mastered all the rules, because you won't be allowed to make an illegal move; the software won't permit it. Most people can figure out how to play or replay games without any instruction, because most of the software used to play is easy to master.

You may be under the impression that chess is a slow game, taking hours to play. Most online games allow each player only a total of three to 15 minutes per player for the entire game. So, you can choose to play a game that will end quite quickly, or take a half-hour at most. Even longer games are available, but they are a rarity. A quick game of chess makes an ideal break from study or work.

Books and Multimedia

The chess world contains many books and resources that you might find interesting. Each of the topics in this book has been the subject of a great deal of literature. After getting a taste in this book, I hope you'll want to explore some topics in greater depth. I'm going to mention some of them in groups, so that you can easily find topics you'd like to learn more about. I'll cite just the title and author, because chess books have gone through many editions with many different publishers, and the best way to find copies of these books, or excerpts online, is to do an Internet search including the title and author.

There are thousands of chess books available for purchase, and thousands more that are no longer in print but can be found at secondhand bookshops. It is difficult to determine by title alone whether a book is written at a level that's appropriate for your own background in chess. Unless you're a highly accomplished player, it is important to select books that feature a lot of text, and aren't filled with a bunch of symbols that look like hieroglyphics. Fortunately, such books are available in abundance.

Chess History

For a modern, detailed account of the history of the game, I recommend *Chess: The History Of The Game* by Richard Eales. If you are interested in the history of the chess pieces themselves, *Chess In Old Russia* by I.M.Linder, and Gareth Williams's *Masterpieces: The Architecture Of Chess*, are fascinating reading. One of the most interesting books on chess history is *Birth of the Chess Queen*: a history by Marilyn Yalom.

All About the Openings

Chess openings have been the subject of study for many centuries, and there is an enormous quantity of literature on the subject. There is now so much information available on opening strategy that it isn't possible even to describe all of the main openings in a single volume. I've written a trilogy of books, adding up to more than 2000 pages, just briefly describing all of the openings. So, you can browse through *Standard Chess Openings*, *Gambit Chess Openings*, and *Unorthodox Chess Openings*, to get a taste of each opening. These books do involve some complicated analysis, and don't really provide enough information for you to actually play an opening; they are meant as aides for choosing which openings to study. You can turn to specialized literature on almost any individual opening. As a compromise, you can look at books like my *World Champion Openings*, which discusses how the best players approach the decisions on opening strategy.

Some authors have bundled together a set of opening strategies presenting what is called an opening repertoire. In these single volumes you can find all the advice you need to play that particular set of openings as either White or Black. There are even books that offer a complete repertoire for both sides. If you happen to play, or are seriously considering playing, a particular opening, these books can provide invaluable tips that you can use to improve your results. If you're just starting out in the game, I naturally recommend my own book, *First Chess Openings*. But any book written specifically for beginners will help, provided that lots of the reasons for each move are included.

Of course I mention my own work, but frankly, it is important to shop around to find authors who can best communicate the information you need at your current stage of chess understanding. Some people learn best from encyclopedic works that provide deep analysis and very little explanation; others benefit from more explanation and do not want to have to absorb hundreds of variations. Many amateur players rely on openings with a high surprise value, and are not concerned how the game might turn out if they're playing against grandmasters. Keep in mind that more recent books will have up-to-date information, while older classics may offer unsurpassed explanations.

Chess Strategy and Tactics

When it comes to strategy and tactics, life is simpler. Frankly, almost any book on tactics will do. Tactical skills are developed by putting your mind to work solving puzzles. If you are just starting out, you'll want a general introduction to the types of tactics that are available. You'll want to see not only individual moves, but how the tactical tracts were set up in the context of the game. *Killer Chess Tactics*, written by Grandmaster Raymond Keene, Grandmaster Leonid Shamkovich and me, is one such book. However, any book that can get you seriously analyzing positions and solving puzzles will greatly improve your game. In most books, the puzzles are presented with just a brief hint or no hint at all. Books by the English Grandmaster Chris Ward have a clever twist. He presents several different plausible descriptions of what's going on in the position, and it's up to you to figure out which logic best fits the concrete analysis of the position. Many of my younger students love that approach. Once again, I recommend that you go to a bookstore and simply take a look at what's on offer. You'll quickly find some books that meet your needs.

Strategy is a different matter altogether. Making long-term strategic decisions is a skill that is not easy to acquire. The best way to study chess strategy, in my opinion, is to play through games of the greatest players, especially when accompanied by thoughtful and clear explanations of the thinking behind the moves. Your choice of books will greatly depend on your own level of play. If you can handle them, the monumental series of books by Garry Kasparov, *Garry Kasparov on My Great Predecessors*, covering the play of all of his predecessors as world champion, will provide a deep understanding of chess strategy. There are also many books devoted to just the topic of strategic thinking in chess, but the books written by world champions themselves stand out as exceptional. The writings of the earlier world champions are much more accessible, as they tend to involve more commentary and less analysis in the form of alternative sequences of moves. To see how modern strategic thinking has changed over the years, John Watson's *Secrets of Modern Chess Strategy* is a wonderful read, though you'll need to be at least an intermediate player to get the most benefit from it. A good introduction for beginners is John Nunn's *Understanding Chess, Move By Move*.

It is customary to mention various classic books, but as John Watson has shown, there is much to criticize in the older books, and chess thinking has changed quite a bit. So I suggest that the classics be read only after a good, general introduction to the topic of chess strategy.

Relive Famous Tournaments

From the very first international chess tournament onwards, books have been written to commemorate major chess events. They not only include all of the games, often with commentary by the players themselves, but also have photographs and stories, even, sometimes, the menus from the opening and closing ceremonies. Often these books have been written by one of the players, or at least have contributions from players. You can play through every game of the tournament from start to finish, enjoying all of the insights, often delivered with wit and humor. Reading the commentaries, you can quickly see how much the game of chess has changed over the years. Often, opening strategies that are now considered quite acceptable for professional use, and are even played at the world championship level, are disparaged and insulted in the notes by classical players. Many of the best of these books are in foreign languages, especially German, but there are a few wonderful books that have been translated, and even some originally written in English. Unfortunately, even the books in English are difficult to read because they used an entirely different method of chess notation from the one we use today. You will want to look for books that include the words "algebraic version," unless you want to learn how the older notation works.

These days, the most dramatic events, for example, the world championship, tend to be reported quickly, with some minimal game commentaries, and brought to market before the result of the match leaves the public eye. Authors of such books work hard to try to bring the flavor of the event to the public, but even in this age of computer analysis, it isn't possible to do justice to a tournament quickly.

Getting up Close and Personal with the Players

In contrast to the dismal state of modern tournament books, books devoted to the study of individual players are in good shape. I already mentioned Gary Kasparov's magnum opus on his predecessors. In addition, you can find books devoted to all sorts of players, not just the world champions. Many veteran grandmasters write memoirs, in which they present their best and most interesting games, and also many fascinating stories. A great example of this is the book by David Bronstein, *The Sorcerer's Apprentice*. No chess library is complete without a copy of Bobby Fischer's *My 60 Memorable Games*. The entire collected writings of World Champion Mikhail Botvinnik are available. There isn't a significant figure in the chess world who has not been profiled in a book. You will generally find it easier to understand the chess of the players of the romantic and classical ages, so you might want to start with a book on Paul Morphy or Wilhelm Steinitz. There are extensive biographies of each of these players. Returning to Bobby Fischer, his biography, *Profile of a Prodigy*, by Frank Brady, is a wonderful read. There are excellent books on the Polgar sisters and other female stars as well. Even young players get into the act, sometimes just contributing, as in my *Whiz Kids Teach Chess*, but sometimes teen chess stars even write their own instructional book, for example, Alexandra Kosteniuk's *Chess Grandmaster At 14*.

On the Fringes

There are books devoted to all aspects of chess. You can find books filled with nothing but pictures and discussions of chess sets, books about the mathematics of the game, books on the history of computer chess, volumes filled with chess trivia and anecdotes, and books on how to use chess software. Some writers produce large volumes of works on players who are largely unknown and have been more or less forgotten by history.

Often there is a fierce rivalry between such authors, and they frequently try to outdo each other, especially when it comes to printing insulting or embarrassing things about members of the chess community. Some do so in a lighthearted way, for example, *The Even More Complete Chess Addict* by Mike Fox and Richard James, a book that is highly praised even by those subject to their barbs, including me. Others are mean-spirited, focusing on minor or typographic errors in chess books, for example. I think you will most enjoy books by George Koltanowski, a grandmaster who was expert on playing blindfold chess, and one of the great raconteurs of the game.

There have been numerous collections of short fiction and excerpts from literature where chess plays a major role in the plot. *The 64 Square Looking Glass* by Burt Hochberg is a wonderful example of such a compilation. There are many novels in which chess plays a large role, including *The Queen's Gambit* by Walter Titus, John Brunner's *Squares of the City* and Katherine Neville's *The Eight*.

Even though most fringe topics in chess have entire books devoted to the esoteric subjects, there is even more information available online and in chess journals and magazines. You can have some fun by using a search engine and entering the word "chess," together with whatever unlikely terms come to mind.

Chess Instruction

You don't have to be a strong player to enjoy the international world of chess. Most tournaments are either open to all players, or have amateur sections alongside the professional competitions. Because no one wants to enter a competition and lose all of their games, many players turn to teachers, coaches and trainers to improve their play.

A chess teacher usually works only at an elementary level. The instruction includes the rules, basic middlegame and endgame strategy, and perhaps a small opening repertoire. Chess teachers usually work in schools and at special chess camps. A good teacher will be a competitive player, usually rated at least 1700. The instruction will be balanced in all areas of the game, and the openings taught will be standard.

Many teachers prefer to teach "trappy" openings designed to bring quick victories against inexperienced competition, but this is not in the long-term interest of the student, because sooner or later, regular opponents learn to avoid the traps, and learning a new set of openings is a lot of work. A good teacher will build a solid foundation of openings that are reliable.

A chess coach has a different task. The coach usually works with a student only during a tournament, and perhaps for a while before and after the event. There is no time to address many of the player's weaknesses. The coach prepares the student for specific openings and opponents, working within the limitations of the student's ability. The goal is to optimize results in competition, not necessarily to raise the level of the player's game significantly.

A good coach will spend some time working on endgames, because that is the hardest stage of the game to master. The coach will not try to radically change the student's opening repertoire in a short period of time, but will try to patch holes and leaks that could lead to disaster. The coach must also offer psychological support. Young players often have difficulty rebounding from a bad game and shattered confidence.

Chess training is the most intensive and expensive form of instruction. A trainer provides regular lessons and coaching, and works to eliminate weaknesses and strengthen overall play. Only the most dedicated young players enter chess training programs. Trainers spend a lot of time on subtle positional concepts and endgames. They work to build a complete, solid opening repertoire, and sometimes prepare special surprises for specific opponents.

Top trainers rarely impose their own opening strategies on their students. They choose from the entire range of respectable openings, picking some to fit the existing skills of the player. Others bring more experience in areas where improvement is needed. The enormous effort required to train young stars usually results in diminished performances by the trainers, whose rankings can suffer. Most successful trainers have been international masters, not grandmasters – though some later went on to become grandmasters.

Some highly ranked grandmasters have become excellent trainers while maintaining their own careers. There are even examples of strong players who have almost entirely abandoned competitive play to become full-time trainers.

Whatever your needs, choosing an appropriate chess instructor is not an easy task, just as it is hard to select a good music teacher or tennis coach. Still, you can usually find someone in your area who can provide good chess instruction. If you just want to enjoy the game and become a better player, you can play in tournaments and take advantage of some free lessons!

How? Play with opponents who are better than you, and make sure to do a post-mortem (post-game analysis) after every serious game. Of course, your "instructors" may not be as qualified as professional trainers, but you are likely to learn some valuable tips. Don't pay too much attention to the opening preferences your opponent might want to foist on you.

Take nothing at face value, but make sure that you understand why your opponent suggests certain moves rather than the ones you played. Perhaps the opponent will be wrong, but there is usually some valuable chess logic to be learned. Naturally, if you get a chance to analyze your game with a strong player, do so! Many scholastic and even open tournaments now offer free analysis of your games by a chess instructor.

When you have played a game and don't understand why you lost, you can also post it on the Internet, at ChessGames (**www.chessgames.com**). Often you'll get several interesting replies, and even masters answer questions from time to time. Chess lessons are becoming more available on the Internet, too.

The Internet and World Wide Web

Entire books have been written on the chess resources available on the Internet, and these are often out-of-date even before they are published. Chess is one of the biggest activities on the Internet, and not just playing games online. Fortunately, there are many resources to keep you up-to-date. Those with good Internet search-ing skills can almost always find whatever they want quite quickly. There is a variety of sites devoted to keeping track of what's interesting on the World Wide Web, and many groups and publications are available for free or by subscription. A few of these are noted in the sidebars.

Throughout this book I've presented some links to established sites that play an important role in the world of chess, but as with everything else on the Internet, you need to look around and see what's available, because things keep changing. Most chess players practice at only one or two online chess clubs, and online chess is a highly competitive business, so there are always new ideas being implemented, and new clubs opening.

As far as the quality of information is concerned, it's generally a matter of "buyer beware." The official newsgroups for chess are filled with trolls and people whose behavior would not be tolerated in any sort of classroom. It is very difficult to dis-tinguish rumor from fact, and you have to take some time before deciding whether what you are reading is from a credible source.

One popular activity on the Internet is raising an allegation that a particular game, tournament, or even world championship match has been fixed. Such allega-tions are almost always without merit, though historically, there are much discussed controversies that have not yet been settled. Still, any time you see an accusation of cheating on the Internet, it is best to assume that it is false. Many excellent players, writers, organizers, and other officials have been falsely maligned, and it is so com-monplace that the majority don't even bother to respond to such allegations.

The amount of misinformation out there is enormous. While watching a game online, for example, you might see people post suggestions for improving your play that seem quite reasonable. They suggest that certain openings would be more appropriate for a player of your level. However, you have absolutely no way of knowing whether this advice comes from someone qualified to give it, or just some self-appointed know-it-all.

Be especially wary of those who promise that they know a way for you to improve your chess rating considerably in a very short period of time. There is no substitute for hard work and study. Remember, what works for someone else may not work for you. If you see an interesting suggestion, try it. Just don't be angry if it doesn't work for you.

One of the great benefits of the Internet is that most players are easily available by e-mail, and can be contacted either directly or through a web page. Even when players take measures to keep the public from knowing the nickname or "handle" they use for online play, they rarely work. So you can actually send messages to players, event organizers, and writers. Personally, I'm grateful when a reader con-tacts me to ask a question about something in one of my books, because the mere fact that the question has to be asked means that I slipped up and didn't present the information as clearly as possible. However, I can use this feedback to improve future editions of the book in question, and to improve my writing overall. I get very few attack letters, because people who just want to hurl insults prefer to do so in the large public forums such as newsgroups, and they only rarely dare to spew directly at an author or player.

On the flip side, celebrity in the chess world comes at a price ---- the same price that is paid by professional athletes and entertainers, except that it comes without all of the huge financial benefits those others enjoy. As with sports, it's all too easy to be an armchair quarterback, especially when you have a computer chess program analyzing every move for you. I'm shocked by many of the comments posted about players and their choice of moves during a game. Fortunately, you can be spared such incivilities when watching games at sites such as the Internet Chess Club, because you can censor anyone posting on the game, and can add them to your blacklist so that you won't see their comments. You can also filter comments on a game to see only the opinions of players who have official chess titles. One can only hope that in future online chess, spectators will be a better-behaved group.

The growth of the Internet has dramatically changed the world of chess. It has brought the game to the masses in ways never before possible, but the doors of the chess cybercafés are always open, and anyone can walk in. So enjoy all the chess the Internet has to offer, and try to avoid the nasty bits.

The Chess Newspaper Delivered Daily

For those who can't let a day go by without a bit of chess news, there is a daily chess newspaper called Chess Today, which can be obtained at LINK: **www.Chesstoday.net**.

TWIC

Mark Crowther edits the essential weekly web publication *The Week in Chess*, located at **www.chesscenter.com/twic/twic.html**. TWIC covers all major events in the world of chess, and acts as a repository for chess news and the most important chess games played each week.

Weekly Web Update

Chessville is a weekly free webzine devoted to pointing out new and exciting chess resources on the World Wide Web. LINK: **www.chessville.com**. It is a great way to keep informed about the major chess events, while also exploring the interesting fringes of the game.

Biweekly Update

The Chess Chronicle, **www.chesschronicle.org**, comes out every two weeks and includes articles by many leading Grandmasters. I contribute a column on recent events. You can pick up a free sample copy at their website.

Chess City

Chess City, **www.chesscity.com**, is Cardoza Publishing's web site for chess. Here you'll find excerpts from Cardoza's many chess books and original articles found nowhere else.

CHAPTER 16
Closing Thoughts

Well, that ends our little tour of the chess world and related cyberspace. I hope that during your journey you have come across some interesting aspects of chess, and that you'll go on to learn more about the game. At first, playing chess will seem difficult. Then it will get easier, before it seems utterly impossible! Remember, whatever your skill level, you can have a lot of fun playing the game. Perhaps you'll create an artistic sacrifice, or win a prize in competition, or simply apply your improved problem-solving skills to get more out of life. Whatever you are after, the chess community can probably supply it!

INDEX

Abrahamyan, Tatiana *256*

Adams, Michael *28, 251*

adjournments *123*

Akobian, Vladimir *253*

Alekhine, Alexander *34-35, 67-68, 158-159, 239, 242, 276*

Alekseyev, Andrey *246*

algebraic chess notation *112, 120, 298*

Anand, Viswanathan *28, 34-35, 251, 264-265, 271*

arbiter *36, 79, 107-110, 121, 185, 261, 264, 281, 283, 285, 287*

Armageddon *123, 258*

Arrington, LaVar *59*

Ashley, Maurice *105*

Austin Powers 45

backward pawn *189-190, 210*

Bacrot, Etienne *28*

Bad Company 45

Baghdad *23-24, 245*

Baramidze, David *246*

Bedazzled 45

Bedlam Hospital *280*

Benjamin, Joel *253, 269*

Berlin *169, 269-270*

Bernstein, Osip *181-182*

Betsson *39*

Bilek, Istvan *105*

Bird, Henry *40*

bishop *49, 55*

Bjelica, Dmitri *260*

Black *48-50*

Black Hawk Down 45

Blackburne, Joseph Henry *279*

Blackburne's Mate *89*

Blade 45

Blade Runner 45

Blazing Saddles 45

Bled *186*

blindfold chess *265, 279, 299*

blitz chess *124, 265*

blockade *195-197*

blocking *72, 176*

Boden's Mate *90*

Bogart, Humphrey *20*

Bond, James *148*

Bonus Socius *241*

books on chess *295-299*

Botvinnik, Mikhail *34, 240, 298*

boxing *109*

breakthrough *231*

Bronstein, David *124, 148-150, 298*

Browne, Walter *211, 256*

Buckle, Henry *40*

Buddhism *23*

Bulgaria *28, 35, 250*

Bundesliga *263*

Byrne, Donald *233*

caffeine *263*

Caliph *23-24*

Cambodia *22*

Cambridge *280*

Candidate Master *30*

Capablanca, Jose Raul *34-35, 181-182, 198, 276, 278*

Capablanca's Rule *211*

capture-checkmate *171*

capture-checks *166-171, 184, 229, 234*

Carlsen, Magnus *246, 248-249, 265*

Carroll, Lewis *66*

casino *265, 271*

Casper 45

Catherine the Great *58*

castling *25, 52, 74-79, 114, 129-130, 186*

center *128-129*

Charlemagne *23, 53*

chaturanga *22*

cheating *108, 283, 302*

check *69-72*

checkmate *25, 50, 51, 73-74, 88-101, 115*

Chess Assistant *293*

chess clock *87, 121-123, 291-292*

chess club *29, 31, 259, 273, 276-277, 289, 295*

chess programs *42, 273, 274*

Chess Base *293*

chessboard *48*

ChessGames.com *301*

Chessmaster *180*

Chessville *304*

Chicago *271*

China *23, 246*

Christiansen, Larry *143-144, 255*

Chronos (chess clock) *292*

coach *300-301*

coffeehouses *26*

combination *165, 287*

Commonwealth *271*

communism *26, 258*

compensation *182-183, 233, 234*

composition *66, 67*

computer *67, 108, 123, 134, 180, 248, 252, 265, 269, 288, 289, 291, 293-295*

Confucius *22*

Conquest *25*

Copenhagen *163*

Corus *249, 264-265*

counterattack *19*

Cozio's Mate *91*

creativity *18, 134, 180*

Crowther, Mark *303*

Cuba *35, 249*

Damiano Bishop Mate *91*

Damiano's Mate *90*

database *15, 31, 39, 120, 133*

Dawn of the Dead 45

decoy *155-157, 159*

Defense *183-188*

DeFirmian, Nick *254*

Deflection *155-157, 159, 165*

Deschapelles, Alexandre *52*

development *131*

Discovered *145-152, 171, 172, 176, 202, 230, 235*

Divinsky, Nathan *31*

Dortmund *245, 265*

Dragon (opening) *127*

draw *16, 86-87, 103-106, 215-216, 220-221, 258, 281-282*

drug testing *35, 248, 263-264*

Dubai *245*

Duchamp, Marcel *35, 239*

Dufresne, Jean *169*

Dzindzichashvili, Roman *59*

Eales, Richard *295*

Edinburgh *279*

Elo rating scale *29-31, 249, 294*

Elo, Arpad *29, 31*

en passant *62-64, 83*

endgame *29, 162, 213-221, 231-233, 242*

Epaulette Mate *92*

Euwe, Max *34, 35, 136, 158, 276*

Evergreen Game *169-171*

Exchange (piece value) *84-86*

Fairchild, Morgan *20*

Farsi *25*

FIDE *21, 26, 30-35, 108, 245, 275*

FIDE Master *30, 32*

Filipowicz, Andrzej *262*

Fine, Reuben *59, 147, 182, 279*

Finegold, Ben *255*

Fischer, Robert J. (Bobby) *19, 26, 34, 42, 148, 233-237, 240, 245, 259, 276, 289, 298*

Fishman, Jon *21*

flank *129, 232*

Fool's Mate *98-99, 115*

forfeit *87, 107, 122, 285, 287*

fork *141-143, 146, 150, 154, 156, 157, 193, 209, 238*

formation *125, 131, 182, 191, 192*

Frankenstein-Dracula (Opening) *127*

Franklin, Benjamin *16*

Fried Liver (opening) *127*

From Russia With Love *148*

Front, The *45*

gambit *131-133, 183, 228, 296*

Gausdal *245, 269*

George of the Jungle *45*

Georgia, Republic of *57*

Gibraltar *270, 271*

ginkgo biloba *263*

Goletiani, Rusudan *256, 257*

Grandmaster *19, 20, 30, 31, 57, 109, 243, 246*

Granger, Hermione *225, 227*

Greco's Mate *93*

Greece *244*

Greek Gift *229-230*

Grigoriyev *67-68, 242*

Grischuk, Alexander *249*

hanging *197*

Harikrishna, Pentala *246*

Harry Potter and the Sorcerer's Stone *45, 225*

Harun Al Rashid *245*

Hastings *105, 202, 245, 268*

Hawaii *27, 271*

Hercules in New York *45*

Hippodrome *261*

Hochberg, Burt *299*

Holland *158, 249, 250, 264*

Hollywood *20*

Hort, Vlastimil *105*

Hungary *28, 35, 246, 250*

Ibragimov, Ildar *253*

Immortal Game *117-120*

Incas *53*

increment *122-124*

Independence Day *45*

International Master *30, 31, 32, 225, 267, 301*

internet *23, 30, 31, 294, 301-303*

isolated pawn *195-197*

Isouard, Count *138-140*

Ivanchuk, Vassily *28*

Ivanov, Alexander *255*

j'adoube *111-112, 283*

Jadoubevich *283*

Johannessen, Leif *248*

Kaidanov, Grigory *252*

Karjakin, Sergei *246*

Karpov, Anatoly *26, 34, 79, 112, 143-144, 240, 245, 261, 276*

Kasimdzhanov, Rustam *34*

Kasparov, Garry *18,19, 28, 31, 33-34, 108, 129, 211, 240, 245, 260, 261, 264-265, 269, 273, 278-279, 284, 286*

Kass, Carmen *41*

Keene, Raymond *31, 278, 296*

Khalifman, Alexander *34, 248*

Khmer *25*

Kieseritzky, Lionel *117-118*

King *49, 50-53, 69-71, 74*

kingside *75, 78, 83, 114, 129, 186, 210*

Kmoch, Hans *104*

Knight *49, 58-59*

knockout *32, 33, 245, 258, 268*

Knudsen, John *280*

Koltanowski, George *279, 299*

Koneru, Humpy *246*

Korchnoi, Viktor *79, 245, 248*

Kosteniuk, Alexandra *41*

Krabbé, Tim *67*

Kramnik, Vladimir *19, 28, 33, 34, 108, 134, 250, 262*

Kudrin, Sergei *252*

La Bourdonnais, Louis Charles Mahe De *52*

Lakdawala, Cyrus *255*

Larsen, Bent *105*

Las Vegas *29, 40, 45, 271*

Lasker, Emanuel *34, 131, 151-154, 180, 276*

leagues *262, 263*

Legall's Mate *94*

Leko, Peter *28, 250*

Lenin, Vladimir *247*

Leningrad *261*

Letterman, David *259*

Levitsky, Stefan *237-239*

Lewis, Lennox *19*

Libya *245*

Linares *33, 245, 265*

Linder, I.M. *295*

Lolli's Mate *94*

London *19, 26, 34, 53, 117, 127, 244, 260, 261, 273, 276, 277, 279, 288*

luck *32, 211, 220, 258*

Malta *36, 245, 263*

Mamedyarov, Shakhriyar *246*

Marshall, Frank *173-177, 237-239*

Master *30, 31, 32, 42, 213, 277-279*

mate *73, 241*

Matulovic, Milan *283*

Mazatlan *20*

McShane, Luke *248*

Mechanics' Institute Chess Club *276-277*

Menchik, Vera *57*

Merano *245*

middlegame *133, 135-212, 228, 229*

Mieses, Jaques *213*

Milman, Lev *254*

Minneapolis *36, 271*

Monaco *173*

Montezuma *53*

Moreau, Colonel *173, 177*

Morozevich, Alexander *249*

Morphy, Paul *53, 138-140, 298*

Morphy's Mate *95*

Muhammad, Stephen *257*

Naiditsch, Arkade *246*

Nakamura, Hikaru *19, 246, 257, 274*

Napoleon *53*

National Master *30*

Natural Born Killers 45

Navara, David *246*

New York *79, 109, 233, 243, 276*

Nimzowitsch, Aron *163-165, 196, 199*

Norway *246, 249*

Norwood, David *125*

Notation (*see* algebraic chess notation)

Nottingham *245*

Novgorod *245*

Novikov, Igor *254*

Nunn, John *297*

O'Kelly, Count Alberich *79*

Onischuk, Alexander *252*

Opening *125-134, 297*

opening variation *127, 297*

Oregon *43*

pairings *30, 36, 252*

Palestine *36*

Palma de Mallorca *245*

Paris *138*

passed pawn *198-199*

patrons *258-259*

pawn *49, 59-68, 189-201, 209, 213, 220*

pawn structure *189-201*

pawn triangles *191-192, 200*

Pearl of Zandvoort *158-159*

penalties *108*

Perelshteyn, Eugene *255*

Persia *25, 57*

Petropolis *183*

Petrosian, Tigran *34, 114, 276*

Philadelphia *245, 271*

Philidor, Francois *52*

Phish *20-21*

Pillsbury's Mate *96*

pin *137-140, 169, 211*

planning *180-183, 207-212*

Play it Again, Sam 45

Play Misty for Me 45

poisoned pawn *127*

Poland *35, 160*

Ponomariov, Ruslan *28, 34, 250*

post-mortem *287-288, 301*

Prague *33, 270*

prison *43*

prize *27, 30, 36-38, 241, 258, 262, 267-271*

Promotion *65-68, 198-199, 217, 218,*
231-232, 242

Purdy, Cecil *15, 213*

Queen *49, 56-58, 143, 214-215*

queenside *75, 78, 83, 114, 129, 133, 163, 178,*
191, 208

Radjabov, Teimour *246*

Rajasthan *271*

Rambo III 45

Ramirez, Alejandro *246*

rankings *29-40, 108, 249, 267, 294, 301*

rating (*see* Elo Rating)

rating class *30*

Reinfeld, Fred *104, 136*

Renaissance *26*

Renman, Nils *269*

Reshevsky, Samuel *183-185, 278*

resignation *87, 105, 282*

Reti's Mate *95*

Reuben, Stewart *110, 261*

reunification *33*

Reykjavik *245*

Rice, Tim *245, 261*

Rocky VI *45*

rook *25, 49, 54, 130-131*

Roosevelt, Theodore *189*

Rotlevi, George *160-162*

round robin *36, 248-251, 264*

Rubinstein, Akiba *104, 160-162, 245*

Russia *27, 28, 35, 51, 53, 58, 151, 181, 246, 249, 250*

Ruy Lopez (opening) *127*

sacrifice *131, 223-242*

Saemisch, Friedrich *87, 163-165*

Saint-Amant, Pierre *276*

Saltsjöbaden *245*

Sanskrit *25*

Savon, Vladimir *183-185*

Scandinavia *269*

Scheherazade *23, 56*

Schwarzenegger, Arnold *20, 41*

scoresheet *79, 87, 105, 116, 120-121*

Searching for Bobby Fischer *45*

seventh rank *65, 182, 201, 211*

Seventh Seal, The *45*

Seville *245*

Shabalov, Alexander *254*

Shaft 2000 *45*

Shakespeare, William *186*

Shamkovich, Leonid *296*

Shapiro, Daniel *106*

Shirov, Alexei *28, 35, 248, 249*

Shoreline Amphitheater *20*

Short, Nigel *249, 261, 285*

Sicilian Defense *127*

Silman, Jeremy *225-227*

skewer *136, 144-145*

software *30, 291, 292-295, 299*

Sokolov, Ivan *250*

Soltis, Andrew *199*

Sonas, Jeff *31*

Sousse *245*

Southeast Asia *23*

Soviet Union *26, 27, 35, 51, 57*

Spain *20, 28, 35, 57, 249, 265, 270*

Spassky, Boris *26, 34, 148-150, 245, 276*

spectators *107, 109, 237, 282, 285-290, 303*

Spielmann, Rudolf *213*

St. Petersburg *261*

Stalag 17 *45*

Star Wars *45*

Staunton, Howard *49, 53*

Stefanova, Antoaneta *248*

Steinitz, Wilhelm *32, 34, 53, 202-207, 298*

stonewall *199, 201, 210*

strategy *99, 121, 127, 131, 136, 165, 180-182, 195, 213, 296-297*

Stripunsky, Alexander *252, 257*

studies (endgame) *242*

Superfly *45*

Superman II *45*

supertournament *33, 245, 249, 264, 286*

Svidler, Peter *250*

Swahili *26*

Swallow-Tail Mate *97*

Sweden *269*

Swiss System *252-257, 268*

Switzerland *285*

tactic *135-136, 138, 145, 150, 155, 165-166, 296-297*

Tal, Mikhail *34, 186-188, 223, 239*

teams *35, 262-263, 264*

Thatcher, Margaret *261*

The Luzhin Defense *45*

Thessaloniki *245*

Three Musketeers, The *45*

tiebreak *123-124, 258, 263*

Timofeyev, Artiom *246*

Titus, Walter *299*

Topalov, Veselin *28, 33, 34, 35, 250*

touch-move *111-112, 283*

tournament *26, 30, 32-33, 36, 86, 105, 107-124, 248-259, 267-271, 286-287, 297-298*

trainers *36, 262, 299-301*

traps *85, 128, 213, 300*

Tripoli *245*

Tunis *283*

Turing test *293*

TWIC (The Week In Chess) *248, 303*

Twins *45*

Ukraine *28, 35, 246, 250*

unorthodox openings *296*

USCF (United States Chess Federation) *31*

Van Wely, Loek *250*

vegetarians *36*

Vienna *127*

Von Bardeleben, Kurt *202-207*

wagering *39-40*

Waikiki *27*

Washington, George *44*

Watson, John *297*

weakness *86, 131, 133, 135, 181, 182, 186, 189, 190, 209-210*

White *48-50*

Wijk aan Zee *143, 245, 249, 264*

Wolf, Heinrich *104*

World Championship *19, 20, 26-27, 30, 32-34, 36, 56, 108-109, 158, 245, 262, 264*

World Chess Federation *21. 27, 31-32, 34, 112, 275*

wrestling *20, 29, 131, 136*

X-Men *15, 45*

x-ray *144-145*

Xiangzhi, Bu *246*

Yalom, Marilyn *295*

Yerevan *245*

Yugoslavia *186*

Zahar, Efimenko *246*

Zandvoort *158*

zugzwang *162-165, 241, 242*

Zukertort, Johannes *32, 276*